The Quilt I.D. Book

THE QUILT I.D. BOOK

4,000 Illustrated and Indexed Patterns

Judy Rehmel

Prentice Hall Press • New York

Published by Prentice Hall Press
A Division of Simon & Schuster, Inc.
Gulf + Western Building
One Gulf + Western Plaza
New York, NY 10023

PRENTICE HALL PRESS is a trademark of Simon & Schuster, Inc.

Library of Congress Cataloging-in-Publication Data
Rehmel, Judy.
The quilt I.D. book.

Bibliography: p.
Includes index.
1. Quilting—Patterns.   2. Quilts—Identification.
I. Title.
TT835.R426   1986   746.9′7′0410973   86-9417
ISBN 0-13-161324-3

Manufactured in the United States of America

10 9 8 7 6 5 4 3 2 1

First Edition

Through the patchwork of the years, from the evolution of the simple patchwork utilitarian quilt to the quilt's current status as a work of art; from the frontier housewife to the professional designer; from my heritage of quilting and the quilters who have touched my life and from my family have come the knowledge and inspiration to produce this work. Thanks is not enough . . . but it is all I have.

Contents

Introduction

Pieced quilt patterns, uniquely American, born out of necessity and fostered by the need to express beauty, have artistically come of age. The names of the creators of the first quilt patterns have been lost to the ages, but every work of art, including a quilt, deserves a name. Just as every artist has the right to name a painting or sculpture, so every quilter has the right to name a quilted creation. Quilts today are works of art that appeal to our sense of beauty and offer an infinite variety of design with respect to color, form, texture, and overall effect. Yet quilts are seldom marked with essential information such as the pattern name, the maker, and the date the quilt was created. This raises the inevitable question—"What is the name of this quilt pattern?"

Helping to identify traditional pieced quilt patterns is the purpose of this quilt key. Identification of more than 4,000 patterns has been simplified by separating the designs into 15 basic categories and, when necessary, subcategories. The method of classification is based on biological keys used for identifying trees, wildflowers, and birds.

After investigating and examining thousands of quilt patterns, I have learned that some patterns have never been given names. The lack of a name is not reason enough to exclude that pattern from this work. Therefore, patterns without names that have appeared elsewhere in print were designated here as "unknown." In time, names will probably be found for many of them.

Just what constitutes a different quilt pattern is not always easy to determine. Some considerations are:

1. *Number of different fabrics used in a block.* Some patterns may have only two contrasting pieces of fabric used in their design. A block using more fabrics but the same number of pieces constitutes a new pattern and quite possibly has a different name. A variation in the arrangement of colors was also designated by a different pattern.

2. *Size, shape, and number of pieces in a block regardless of the visual design.* The way the piecing is done in one block may be very different from how it is done in another block even though the visual designs

appear identical. In the examples below, each pattern probably was given a different name.

3. *Arrangement of pieces or sections within a block.* Pieces may be "pointing" in one direction for one pattern and in the opposite for another. In some cases the names are different.

4. *Size of pieces.* A great contrast in the size of pieces makes for different patterns.

5. *Optical illusion as to what constitutes a block.* When set together, some blocks appear much different.

6. *Design position within the block.* Designs may be alike but turned within the block. The examples below are given different names.

7. *Technique.* All patterns in this collection of 4,000 are primarily pieced. Some include small appliquéd pieces such as stems, handles, and the like. These patterns are indicated by "pieced and appliquéd."

How to Use the Quilt Key

1. Look carefully at the quilt pattern you want to identify and examine the individual block. Determine the major category (see A to N in Quilt Key) to which the quilt pattern belongs.
2. If the quilt pattern falls in categories G, H, I, J, L, M, or N, turn directly to the page indicated on the key and look through the patterns in that category.
3. If the quilt pattern falls in B, D, E, F, or K, go to the subcategories and find the appropriate number. Turn to the page indicated and look through the patterns in that category.
4. If the quilt pattern falls in A or C, find the appropriate numbered category in the major section and, if applicable, the small letter category. Turn to the page indicated and look through the numbered category indicated.
5. If you do not find the correct match, take another look at the quilt block. Many designs could fall into more than one category. Try again. You have 4,000 chances of naming your quilt pattern!

For example:

This block is made up of four sections, all alike. Refer to section C on the Quilt Key. There are dividers in between, however, so refer to subcategory C.2. The sections are all alike, so C.2.a. is the final category. Turn to page 85 and look through patterns 993 to 1164. Pattern 1116—Dove in the Window—is shown here.

This block basically consists of nine patches. See section D. The corner sections are alike, the side sections are alike, and the center has its own distinct pattern. Therefore, 4-4-1 represents the configuration of the block. See subcategory D.2. Turn to page 121 and look through patterns 1415 to 1543. Pattern 1481—Five-patch—is shown here.

This block is one of the star patterns. Refer to section K. It has eight points so K.4. is the correct subcategory. Turn to page 254 and look through patterns 2948 to 3352. Pattern 3036—Shoofly—is shown here. This pattern might also appear as a basic nine-patch; however, it is placed with the stars. Check to see into which other categories a pattern might fit.

Quilt Key

Author's Note

Throughout the history of quiltmaking, the names of quilt patterns have appeared in many different forms. The discrepancies are not surprising, since many of the patterns were named at a time when reading and writing skills were not as common or widespread as they are today. In her research, the author found many variations in spelling, capitalization, and punctuation of the quilt names. Similarly some patterns had more than one name, either in the same source or in two or more different sources.

For the purposes of this book, spelling, capitalization, and punctuation of quilt names have been conformed to one style for consistency (i.e., bow tie always appears as bow tie *not* as bowtie or bow-tie, even if the original researched spelling was one of these variations). However, if an alternate spelling could be interpreted as an alternate name for the pattern, it was retained (see pattern 917: Robbing Peter to Pay Paul and Rob Peter and Pay Paul).

Patterns that were assigned more than one name are footnoted and alternate terms are given at the bottoms of appropriate pages. It should be noted that the main entry, that is, the entry that appears next to the caption, is not necessarily the preferred or most common name for the pattern in any given area of the country. It is simply the first name for the pattern that the author came across in her research.

Quilt Patterns

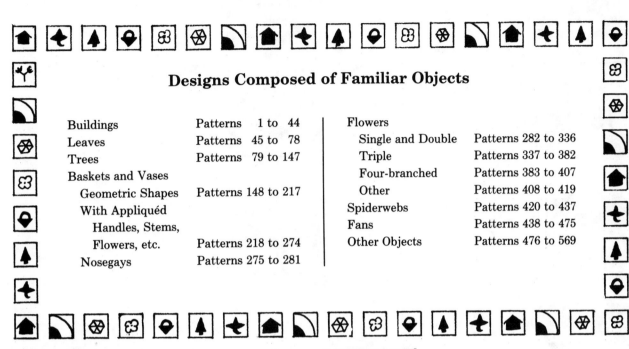

Designs Composed of Familiar Objects

1. Log Cabin

4. Schoolhouse

2. Country Church

5. Schoolhouse Quilt

3. Old Country Church

6. Honeymoon Cottage

 7. Honeymoon Cottage

 13. Log Cabin

 8. Honeymoon Cottage

 14. Log Cabin

 9. Old Homestead

 15. Log Cabin

 10. Courthouse Square

 16. Schoolhouse

 11. Album House (pieced and appliquéd)

 17. Schoolhouse

 12. Schoolhouse

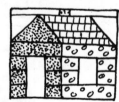 18. Little Red Schoolhouse

 19. Unknown

 20. House

 21. House on the Hill

 22. House

 23. Schoolhouse

 24. Log Cabin

 25. Houses

 26. The Old Homestead

 27. Old Homestead

 28. House

 29. Red Schoolhouse

 30. Unknown

 31. House

 32. Little Red Schoolhouse*

 33. Little Red Schoolhouse

 34. Schoolhouse†

 35. Unknown

 36. Cabins

 37. Red Schoolhouse

 38. Schoolhouse

 39. Schoolhouse

 40. Schoolhouse‡

 41. Houses§

 42. Jack's House

* *Also:* Red Schoolhouse.
† *Also:* Old Homestead.
‡ *Also:* Log Cabin, Old Kentucky Home.
§ *Also:* Old Kentucky Home.

 43. Little Red Schoolhouse

 49. Sweet Gum (pieced and appliquéd)

 44. Village Church

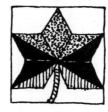 50. Maple Leaf (pieced and appliquéd)

 45. Maple Leaf

 51. Maple Leaf (pieced and appliquéd)

 46. Maple Leaf

 52. Tea Leaf

 47. Sweet Gum Leaf (pieced and appliquéd)

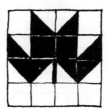 53. Tea Leaf

 48. Sweet Gum Leaf (pieced and appliquéd)

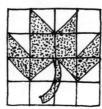 54. Tulip Tree Leaves (pieced and appliquéd)

6

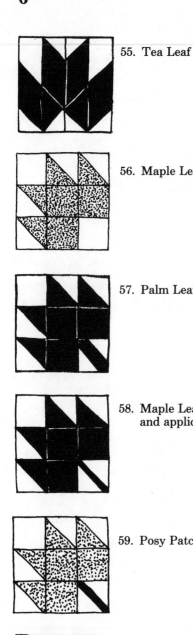
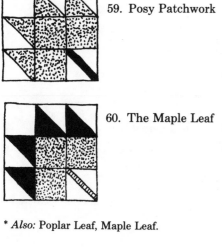

55. Tea Leaf

56. Maple Leaf

57. Palm Leaf*

58. Maple Leaf Quilt (pieced and appliquéd)

59. Posy Patchwork

60. The Maple Leaf

61. Tea Leaves

62. Widow's

63. Hosanna

64. The Four-leaf Clover

65. State of Ohio

66. Maple Leaf

* *Also:* Poplar Leaf, Maple Leaf.

67. Maple Leaf (pieced and appliquéd)

68. Maple Leaf

69. Autumn Leaf

70. Autumn Leaf

71. Unknown

72. Autumn Leaf

73. Autumn Leaf

74. Palm Leaf*

75. Palm Leaf†

76. Palm

77. State of Ohio‡

78. The Reel

Also: Hosanna, Palm Leaves, Hosannah!
† *Also:* Hosanna.
‡ *Also:* Ohio.

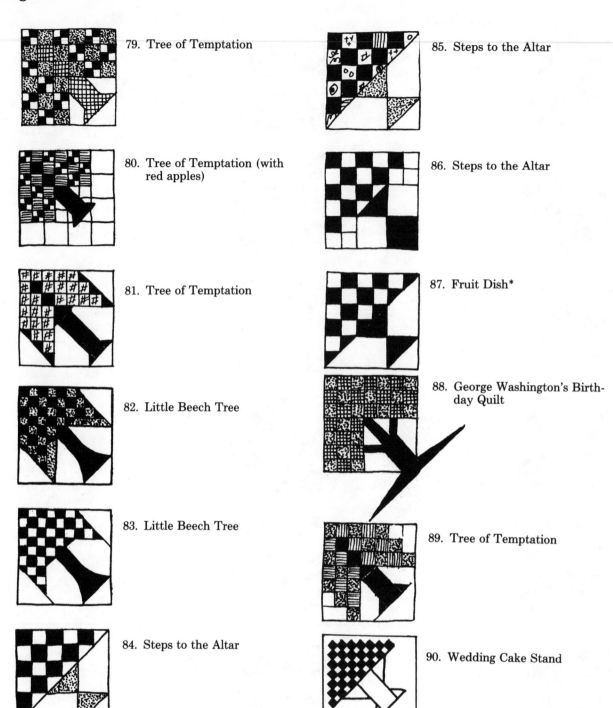

79. Tree of Temptation

80. Tree of Temptation (with red apples)

81. Tree of Temptation

82. Little Beech Tree

83. Little Beech Tree

84. Steps to the Altar

85. Steps to the Altar

86. Steps to the Altar

87. Fruit Dish*

88. George Washington's Birthday Quilt

89. Tree of Temptation

90. Wedding Cake Stand

*Also: Cake Stand.

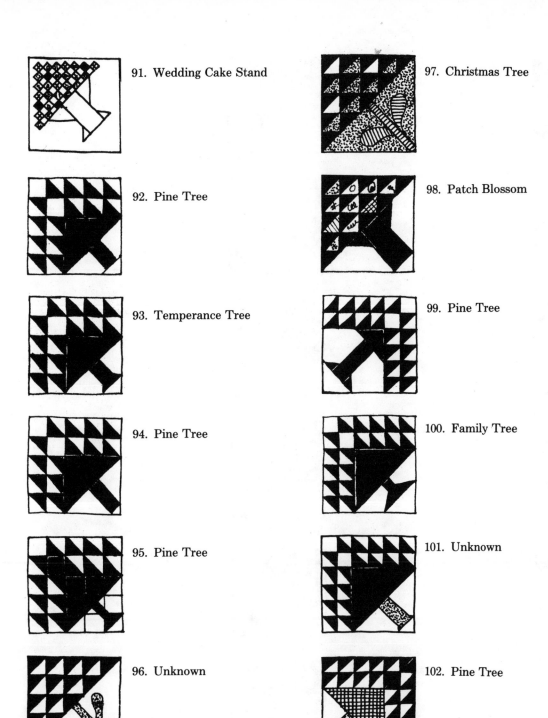

91. Wedding Cake Stand

92. Pine Tree

93. Temperance Tree

94. Pine Tree

95. Pine Tree

96. Unknown

97. Christmas Tree

98. Patch Blossom

99. Pine Tree

100. Family Tree

101. Unknown

102. Pine Tree

 103. Pine Tree

 109. Tree of Life

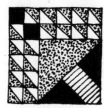 104. Pine Tree

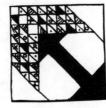 110. Tree of Paradise

 105. Pine Tree

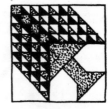 111. Tree of Paradise

 106. Tree of Life (pieced and appliquéd)

 112. Tree of Life

 107. Pine Tree

 113. Pine Tree

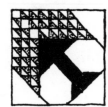 108. Tree of Paradise

 114. Pine Tree

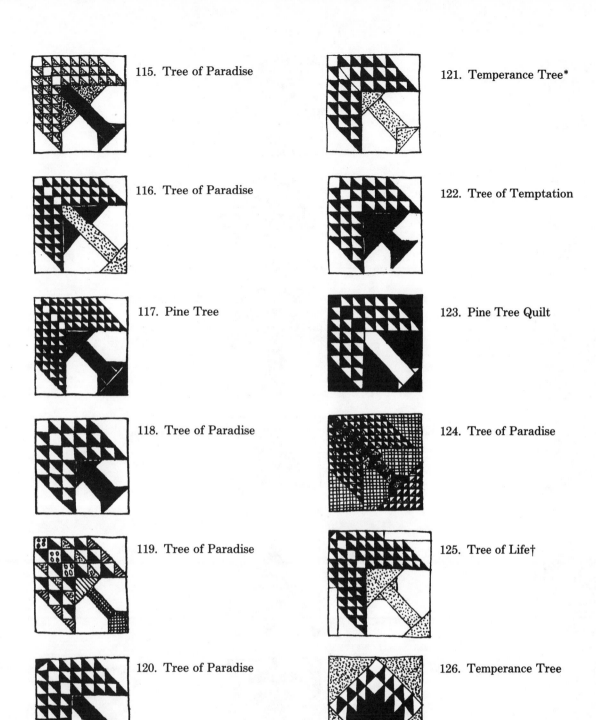

115. Tree of Paradise

116. Tree of Paradise

117. Pine Tree

118. Tree of Paradise

119. Tree of Paradise

120. Tree of Paradise

121. Temperance Tree*

122. Tree of Temptation

123. Pine Tree Quilt

124. Tree of Paradise

125. Tree of Life†

126. Temperance Tree

* *Also:* Pine Tree, Tall Pine Tree.
† *Also:* Christmas Tree.

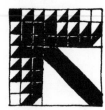 127. Proud Pine

 133. Forbidden Fruit

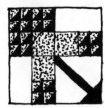 128. Indiana Tulip Tree Block

 134. Forbidden Fruit Tree

 129. Pinetree

 135. Unknown

 130. Live Oak Tree

 136. Pine Tree

 131. Forbidden Fruit Tree

 137. Pine Tree

 132. Peony Block*

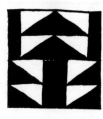 138. Tall Pine Tree

* *Also:* Peony Patch, Piney.

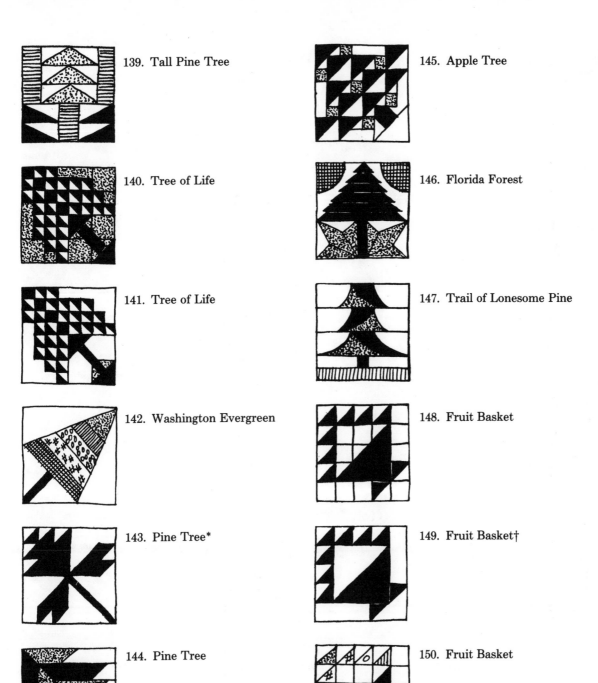

139. Tall Pine Tree

140. Tree of Life

141. Tree of Life

142. Washington Evergreen

143. Pine Tree*

144. Pine Tree

145. Apple Tree

146. Florida Forest

147. Trail of Lonesome Pine

148. Fruit Basket

149. Fruit Basket†

150. Fruit Basket

* *Also:* Weeping Willow, English Ivy.
† *Also:* Basket of Triangles.

 151. Basket

 152. Cake Stand

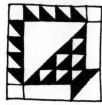 153. Cake Plate

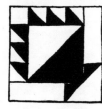 154. Basket

 155. Baskets

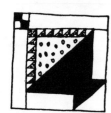 156. Hanging Basket

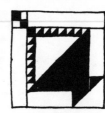 157. Hanging Basket

 158. Fan Basket

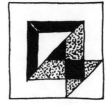 159. Red Basket

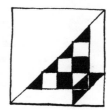 160. Grandmother's Basket

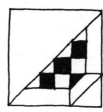 161. Grandmother's Basket

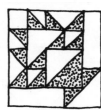 162. Flower Basket

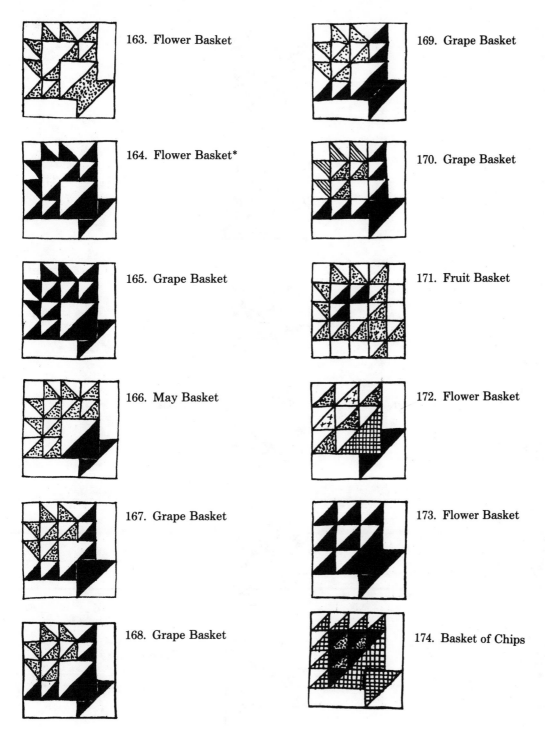

163. Flower Basket

164. Flower Basket*

165. Grape Basket

166. May Basket

167. Grape Basket

168. Grape Basket

169. Grape Basket

170. Grape Basket

171. Fruit Basket

172. Flower Basket

173. Flower Basket

174. Basket of Chips

*Also: Grape Basket.

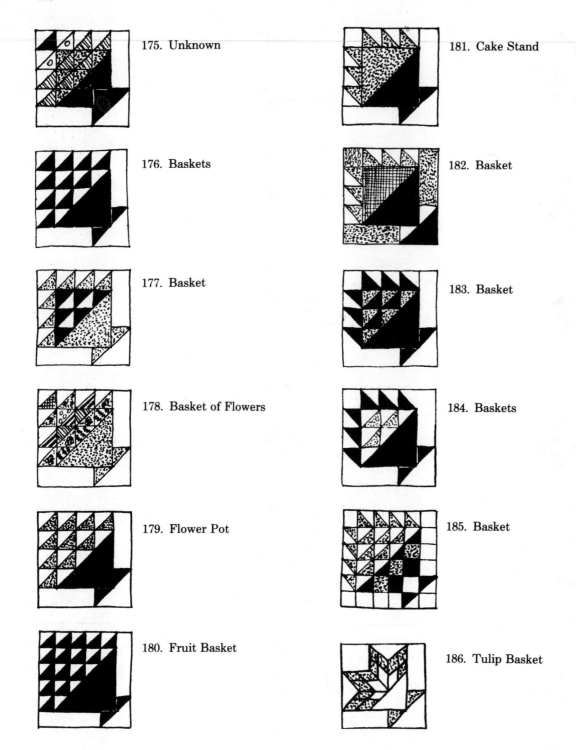

175. Unknown

181. Cake Stand

176. Baskets

182. Basket

177. Basket

183. Basket

178. Basket of Flowers

184. Baskets

179. Flower Pot

185. Basket

180. Fruit Basket

186. Tulip Basket

 187. Tulip Basket

 193. Scrap Basket

 188. Flower Pot

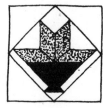 194. Cactus Basket

 189. Flowers in a Basket

 195. Sage Bud†

 190. Tulip Basket

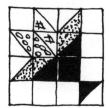 196. Bouquet

 191. A Section of Parquetry*

 197. The Disk

 192. Flower Pot

 198. Basket of Scraps

* *Also:* Hick's Basket.
† *Also:* Bouquet.
‡ *Also:* Scrap Basket.

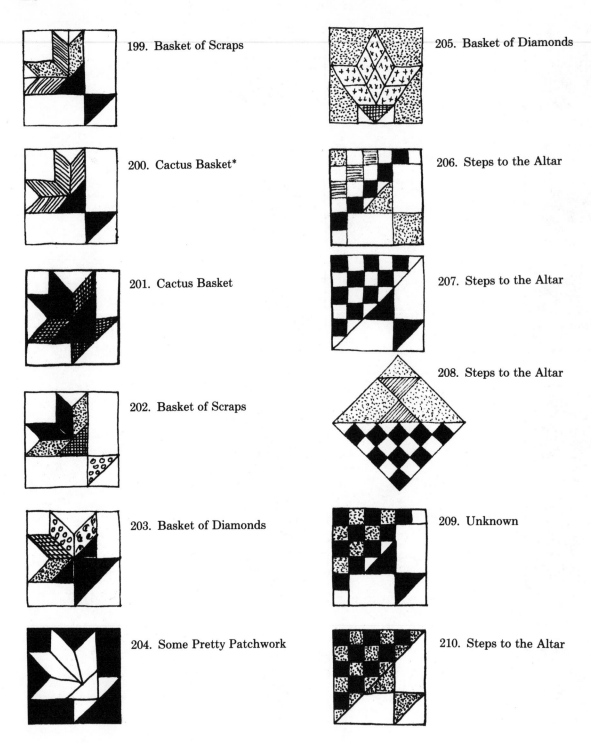

199. Basket of Scraps

200. Cactus Basket*

201. Cactus Basket

202. Basket of Scraps

203. Basket of Diamonds

204. Some Pretty Patchwork

205. Basket of Diamonds

206. Steps to the Altar

207. Steps to the Altar

208. Steps to the Altar

209. Unknown

210. Steps to the Altar

* *Also:* Basket of Scraps, Desert Rose, Texas Rose, Texas Treasure.

 211. Vase of Flowers

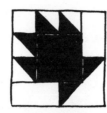 217. Cactus Basket

 212. Tea Basket

 218. The May Basket Quilt
(pieced and appliquéd)

 213. Unknown

 219. Flower Basket (pieced and
appliquéd)

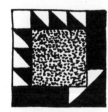 214. Cake Stand

 220. Flower Basket (pieced and
appliquéd)

 215. Leafy Basket

 221. Cherry Basket (pieced and
appliquéd)

 216. Basket Appliqué

 222. Unknown

 223. Unknown (pieced and ap-
pliquéd)

 224. Baby Basket (pieced and
appliquéd)

 225. Miniature Baskets (pieced
and appliquéd)

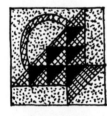 226. Basket (pieced and appli-
quéd)

 227. Unknown (pieced and ap-
pliquéd)

 228. Basket (pieced and appli-
quéd)

 229. Basket Quilt (pieced and
appliquéd)

 230. Cherry Basket Quilt
(pieced and appliquéd)

231. Cherry Basket (pieced and
appliquéd)

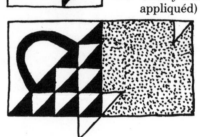

 232. Flower Basket (pieced and
appliquéd)

 233. Basket* (pieced and appli-
quéd)

 234. Basket (pieced and appli-
quéd)

* *Also:* Basket with Appliquéd Handle.

235. Colonial Basket (pieced and appliquéd)

236. Cherry Basket (pieced and appliquéd)

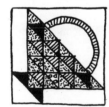

237. Cherry Basket (pieced and appliquéd)

238. Cherry Basket (pieced and appliquéd)

239. Cherry Basket (pieced and appliquéd)

240. Cherry Basket (pieced and appliquéd)

241. Flower Basket (pieced and appliquéd)

242. Bread Basket (pieced and appliquéd)

243. Basket Quilt (pieced and appliquéd)

244. Basket (pieced and appliquéd)

245. Four Little Baskets (pieced and appliquéd)

246. Baskets* (pieced and appliquéd)

* *Also:* Stamp Basket.

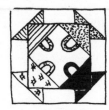

247. Tiny Basket (pieced and appliquéd)

253. Basket and Rose (pieced and appliquéd)

248. Four Little Baskets (pieced and appliquéd)

254. Basket with Leaves (pieced and appliquéd: leaves are quilted)

249. Basket Quilt (pieced and appliquéd)

255. Basket Design (pieced and appliquéd)

250. Basket (pieced and appliquéd)

256. Country House Basket (pieced and appliquéd)

251. Unknown (pieced and appliquéd)

257. Basket and Iris (pieced and appliquéd)

252. Jennie's Basket (pieced and appliquéd)

258. Basket of Flowers (pieced and appliquéd)

 259. Basket (pieced and appliquéd)

 265. Basket of Lilies* (pieced and appliquéd)

 260. The Basket (pieced and appliquéd)

 266. Tulip Basket Quilt (pieced and appliquéd)

 261. Basket of Oranges (pieced and appliquéd)

 267. Garden Basket (pieced and appliquéd)

 262. Garden Basket (pieced and appliquéd)

 268. Springtime (pieced and appliquéd)

 263. Fruit Basket (pieced and appliquéd: arrangement of fruit varies)

 269. Basket of Tulips† (pieced and appliquéd)

 264. Basket of Lilies (pieced and appliquéd)

 270. Basket of Lilies‡ (pieced and appliquéd)

* *Also:* Basket of Tulips.
† *Also:* Basket of Lilies.
‡ *Also:* Basket of Tulips.

 271. Royal Japanese Vase (pieced and appliquéd)

 277. Cornucopia

 272. Tulip in Vase (pieced and appliquéd)

 278. Old-fashioned Nosegay

 273. Tulip Basket (pieced and appliquéd)

 279. The Nosegays

 274. Tulip (pieced and appliquéd)

 280. Cockscomb

 275. Cornucopia

 281. Old-fashioned Nosegay

 276. Bride's Bouquet*

 282. Rose

*Also: Nosegay.

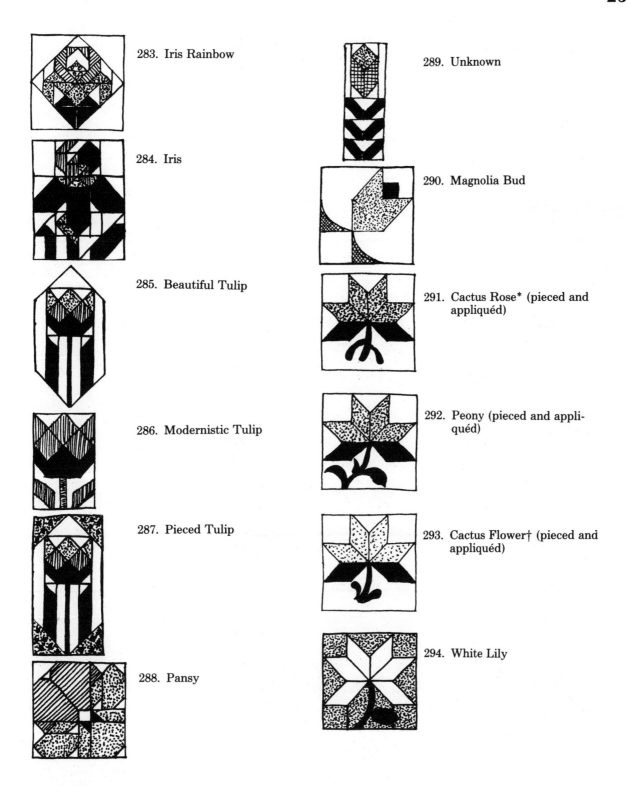

283. Iris Rainbow

284. Iris

285. Beautiful Tulip

286. Modernistic Tulip

287. Pieced Tulip

288. Pansy

289. Unknown

290. Magnolia Bud

291. Cactus Rose* (pieced and appliquéd)

292. Peony (pieced and appliquéd)

293. Cactus Flower† (pieced and appliquéd)

294. White Lily

* *Also:* Peony.
† *Also:* Cactus Rose, Scripture Quilt, Peony.

295. Peony (pieced and appliquéd)

301. Crocus

296. Unknown (pieced and appliquéd)

302. Fleur de Lis

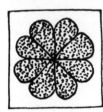

297. Unknown

303. Buttercup

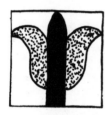

298. Tulip

304. Spring Fancy

299. Pond Lily

305. Water Lily

300. Pieced Tulip

306. Flower of Spring

 307. Calla Lily

 313. Daffodil

 308. Lotus

 314. Dogwood

 309. Sunflower

 315. Carnation

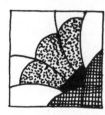 310. Grandmother's Favorite Lily

 316. Nosegay

 311. Star Flower

 317. Crocus

 312. Flower of Friendship

 318. Bell Flower

 319. Field of Daisies*

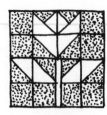 325. Pieced Flower

 320. Field of Daisies

 321. Tulip Garden

 326. Arkansas Meadow Rose (pieced and appliqued)

 327. Arkansas Meadow Rose (pieced and appliquéd)

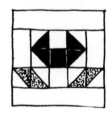 322. Flower Baby Quilt

 328. Windblown Lily (pieced and appliquéd)

 323. Star Flower

 329. The Clover Blossom

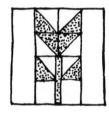 324. Pieced Flower

 330. Unknown (pieced and appliquéd)

* *Also:* Field of Pansies.

 331. Colorado Columbine (center is yo-yo and French knots)

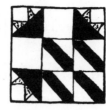 337. Tassel Plant

 332. Harrison Rose

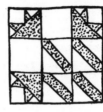 338. Tassel Plant

 333. Star Flower (pieced and appliquéd)

 339. Tulip* (pieced and appliquéd)

 334. Bouquet in a Fan

 340. Unknown (pieced and appliquéd)

 335. Landon Sunflower

 341. Tulip† (pieced and appliquéd)

 336. Trumpet Vine

 342. Tulip (pieced and appliquéd)

* *Also:* Virginia Lily, North Carolina Lily.
† *Also:* Virginia Lily, North Carolina Lily.

343. Pieced-leaf Lily (pieced and appliquéd)

349. Diamond Lily (pieced and appliquéd)

344. Mariposa Lily (pieced and appliquéd)

350. Noonday Lily† (pieced and appliquéd)

345. Virginia Lily* (pieced and appliquéd)

351. Diamond Lily‡ (pieced and appliquéd)

346. Lily Block (pieced and appliquéd)

352. North Carolina Lily§ (pieced and appliquéd)

347. Day Lily (pieced and appliquéd)

353. Double Tulip (pieced and appliquéd)

348. Lily (pieced and appliquéd)

354. North Carolina Lily (pieced and appliquéd)

* *Also:* North Carolina Lily.
† *Also:* Pot of Flowers.
‡ *Also:* North Carolina Lily.
§ *Also:* Mountain Lily, Fire Lily, Wood Lily, Prairie Lily, Noonday Lily, Meadow Lily, Mariposa Lily.

355. Noonday Lily (pieced and appliquéd)

356. Unknown (pieced and appliquéd)

357. Cleveland Lilies (pieced and appliquéd)

358. North Carolina Lily (pieced and appliquéd)

359. Unknown (pieced and appliquéd)

360. Chicago Art Institute Lily (pieced and appliquéd)

361. Antique Shop Tulip* (pieced and appliquéd)

362. Triple Sunflower Quilt (pieced and appliquéd)

363. Triple Sunflower (pieced and appliquéd)

364. Triple Sunflower (pieced and appliquéd)

365. Triple Sunflower† (pieced and appliquéd)

366. Double Peony (pieced and appliquéd)

* *Also:* Double Tulip, Columbus.
† *Also:* Kansas Sunflower.

367. Tulip* (pieced and appliquéd)

368. President's Quilt†

369. Tulip (pieced and appliquéd)

370. Bed of Peonies (pieced and appliquéd)

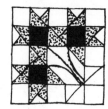

371. Peony (pieced and appliquéd)

372. The Peony (pieced and appliquéd)

373. Cleveland Lilies (pieced and appliquéd)

374. Peony Lily (pieced and appliquéd)

375. Carolina Lily (pieced and appliquéd)

376. Mississippi Pink

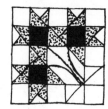

377. Cluster of Stars (pieced and appliquéd)

378. Pineapple

* *Also:* Peony.
† *Also:* Cleveland Tulip.

 379. Meadow Lily* (pieced and appliquéd)

 385. Peony

 380. Basket of Roses (pieced and appliquéd)

 386. Peony§

 381. Peony†

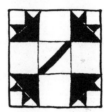 387. WCT Union

 382. Triple Rose (pieced and appliquéd)

 388. Milwaukee's Own

 383. Basket of Lilies

 389. Square and Lily

 384. Basket of Tulips‡

 390. Tulip

* *Also:* Tiger Lily, North Carolina Lily, Wood Lily, Mariposa Lily, Noonday Lily, Pennsylvania Tulip, Mountain Lily, Prairie Lily, Fire Lily.
† *Also:* Lily.
‡ *Also:* Basket of Lilies.
§ *Also:* Maple Leaf.

391. Lily of the Valley

392. Dutch Tulips

393. Lily of the Valley

394. Four Tulips

395. Wandering Foot

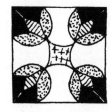396. Wandering Foot

397. Hands All Around

398. Bleeding Heart

399. Bird of Paradise

400. Friendship Knot

401. Tulip

402. The Jackson Star

 403. Peony

 409. Cactus Bud

 404. Painted Daisies

 410. Cactus Flower

 405. Colony Garden Flower

 411. Texas Flower†

 406. Flower Reel* (pieced and appliquéd)

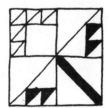 412. Unknown

 407. Poinsettia

 413. Cottage Tulips

 408. Cactus Flower

 414. Cottage Tulip‡

* *Also:* The Posy Quilt.
† *Also:* Texas Treasure.
‡ *Also:* Olive's Yellow Tulip.

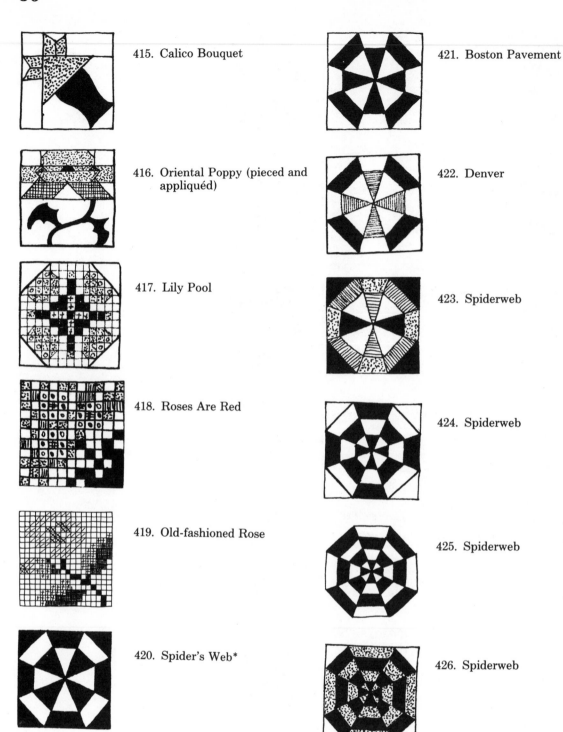

415. Calico Bouquet

416. Oriental Poppy (pieced and appliquéd)

417. Lily Pool

418. Roses Are Red

419. Old-fashioned Rose

420. Spider's Web*

421. Boston Pavement

422. Denver

423. Spiderweb

424. Spiderweb

425. Spiderweb

426. Spiderweb

* *Also:* Spiderweb.

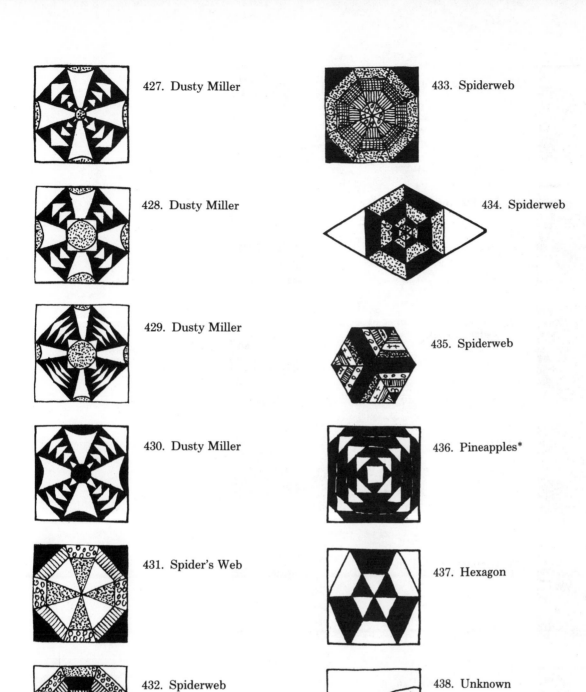

427. Dusty Miller

428. Dusty Miller

429. Dusty Miller

430. Dusty Miller

431. Spider's Web

432. Spiderweb

433. Spiderweb

434. Spiderweb

435. Spiderweb

436. Pineapples*

437. Hexagon

438. Unknown

* *Also:* Wild Goose Chase.

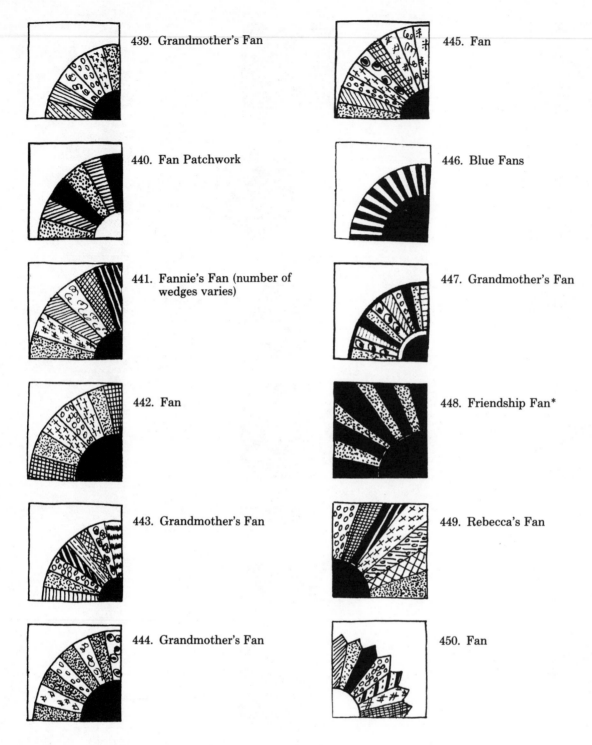

439. Grandmother's Fan

440. Fan Patchwork

441. Fannie's Fan (number of wedges varies)

442. Fan

443. Grandmother's Fan

444. Grandmother's Fan

445. Fan

446. Blue Fans

447. Grandmother's Fan

448. Friendship Fan*

449. Rebecca's Fan

450. Fan

* *Also:* Rebecca's Fan.

 451. Grandmother's Fan

 457. Fan

 452. Milady's Fan

 458. Grandmother's Fan

 453. Flo's Fan

 459. Grandmother's Fan

 454. Flo's Fan

 460. Grandmother's Fan

 455. Fan*

 461. Grandmother's Fan

 456. Alice Brooks

 462. Fan

* *Also:* Flo's Fan.

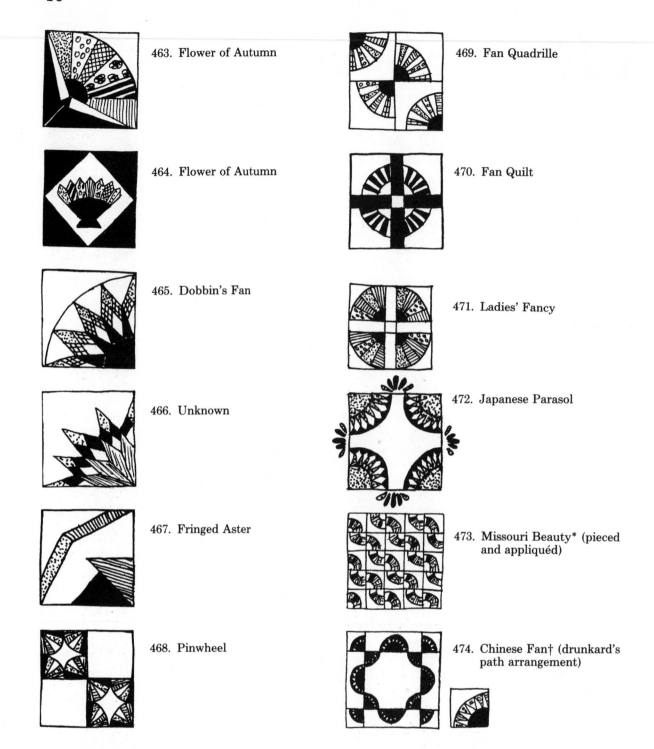

463. Flower of Autumn

469. Fan Quadrille

464. Flower of Autumn

470. Fan Quilt

465. Dobbin's Fan

471. Ladies' Fancy

466. Unknown

472. Japanese Parasol

467. Fringed Aster

473. Missouri Beauty* (pieced and appliquéd)

468. Pinwheel

474. Chinese Fan† (drunkard's path arrangement)

* *Also:* Whig's Defeat, Fannie's Favorite, Grandmother's Engagement Ring.
† *Also:* Fans.

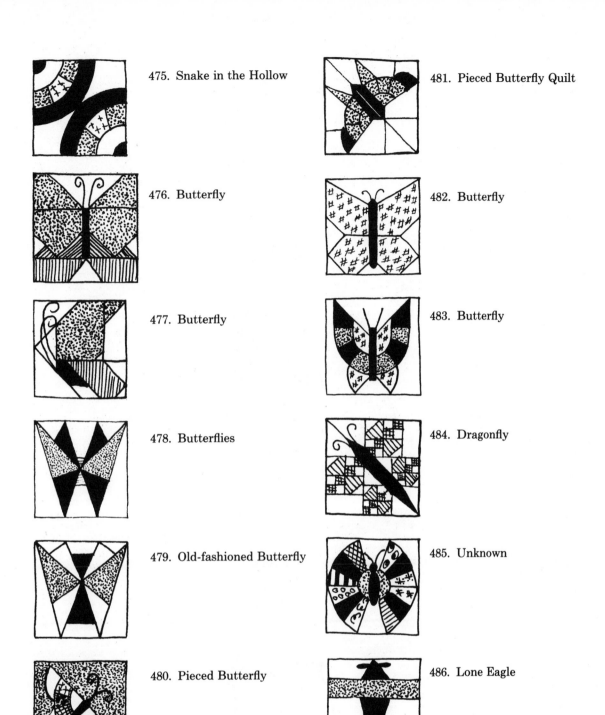

475. Snake in the Hollow

481. Pieced Butterfly Quilt

476. Butterfly

482. Butterfly

477. Butterfly

483. Butterfly

478. Butterflies

484. Dragonfly

479. Old-fashioned Butterfly

485. Unknown

480. Pieced Butterfly

486. Lone Eagle

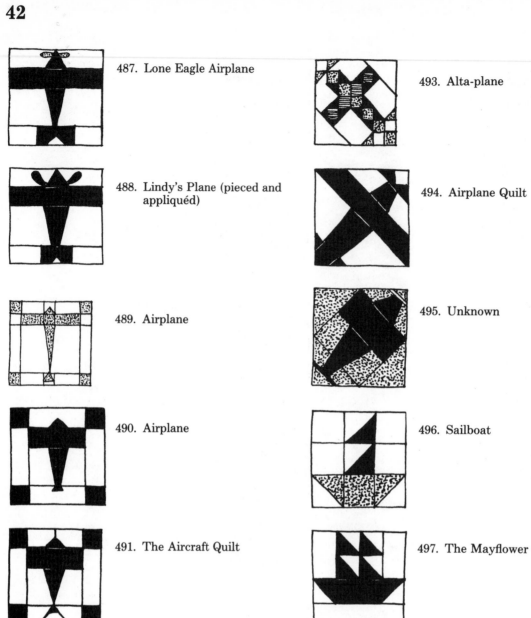

487. Lone Eagle Airplane

488. Lindy's Plane (pieced and appliquéd)

489. Airplane

490. Airplane

491. The Aircraft Quilt

492. Unknown

493. Alta-plane

494. Airplane Quilt

495. Unknown

496. Sailboat

497. The Mayflower

498. Mayflower

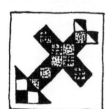

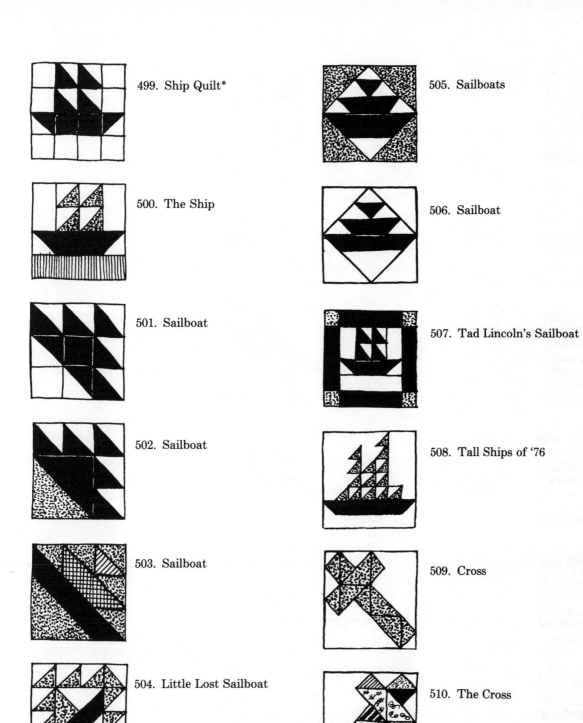

499. Ship Quilt*

500. The Ship

501. Sailboat

502. Sailboat

503. Sailboat

504. Little Lost Sailboat

505. Sailboats

506. Sailboat

507. Tad Lincoln's Sailboat

508. Tall Ships of '76

509. Cross

510. The Cross

* *Also:* Mayflower, Ship of Dreams.

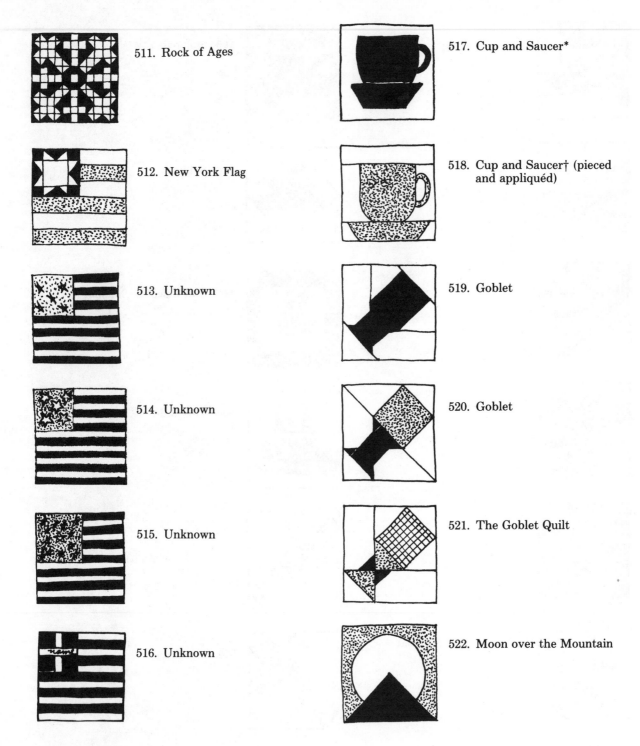

511. Rock of Ages

512. New York Flag

513. Unknown

514. Unknown

515. Unknown

516. Unknown

517. Cup and Saucer*

518. Cup and Saucer† (pieced and appliquéd)

519. Goblet

520. Goblet

521. The Goblet Quilt

522. Moon over the Mountain

* *Also:* Coffee Cups.
† *Also:* Tea Time.

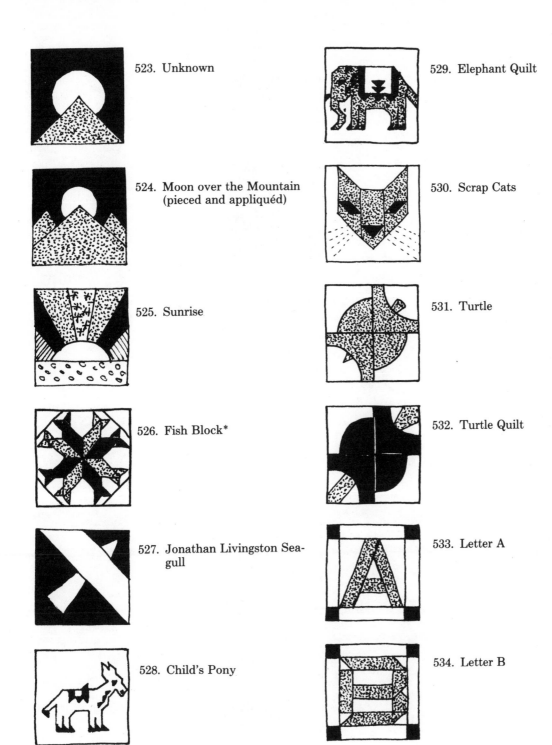

523. Unknown

524. Moon over the Mountain
(pieced and appliquéd)

525. Sunrise

526. Fish Block*

527. Jonathan Livingston Sea-
gull

528. Child's Pony

529. Elephant Quilt

530. Scrap Cats

531. Turtle

532. Turtle Quilt

533. Letter A

534. Letter B

* *Also:* Goldfish, Airplanes, Bass and Trout, Fish, Starfish.

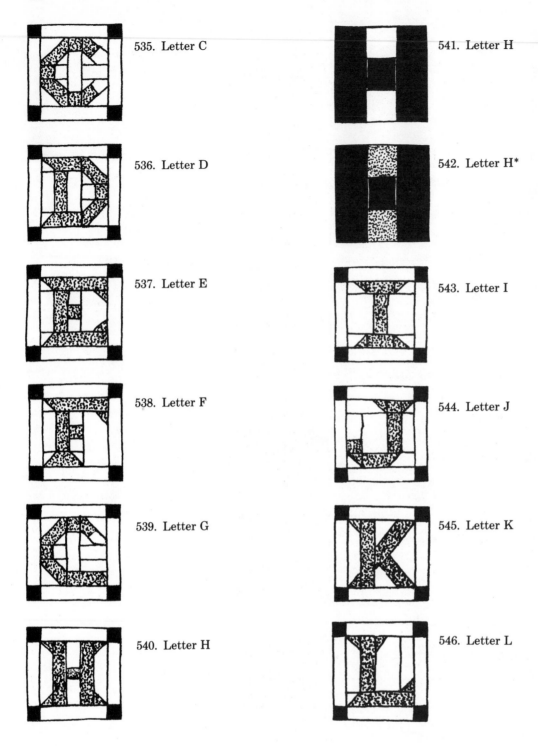

535. Letter C

536. Letter D

537. Letter E

538. Letter F

539. Letter G

540. Letter H

541. Letter H

542. Letter H*

543. Letter I

544. Letter J

545. Letter K

546. Letter L

* *Also*: H.

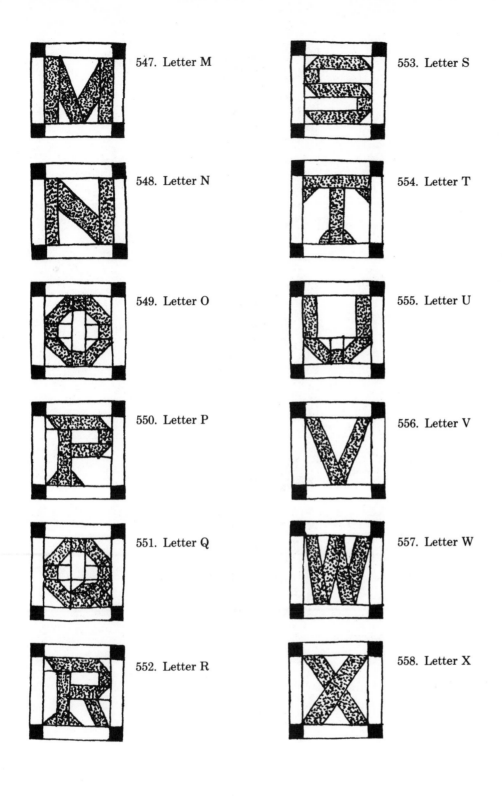

547. Letter M

548. Letter N

549. Letter O

550. Letter P

551. Letter Q

552. Letter R

553. Letter S

554. Letter T

555. Letter U

556. Letter V

557. Letter W

558. Letter X

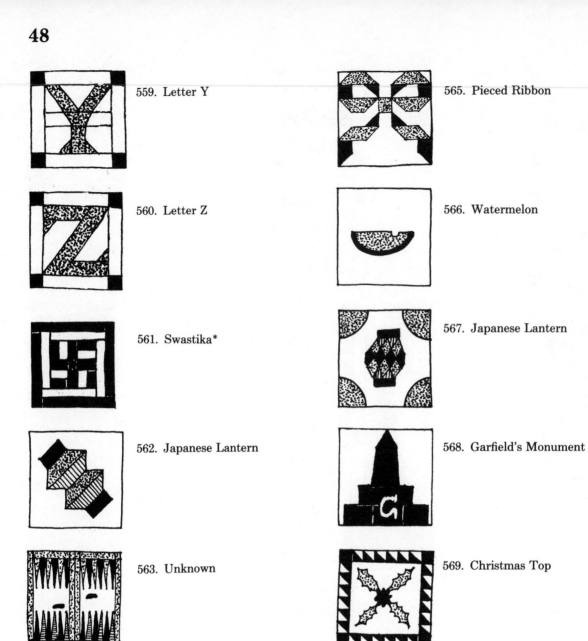

559. Letter Y

560. Letter Z

561. Swastika*

562. Japanese Lantern

563. Unknown

564. Acorn

565. Pieced Ribbon

566. Watermelon

567. Japanese Lantern

568. Garfield's Monument

569. Christmas Top

* *Also:* Pure Symbol of Right Doctrine, Mound Builders, Wind Power of the Osage.

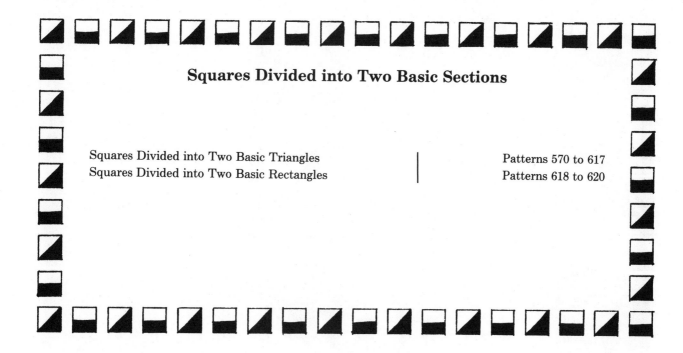

Squares Divided into Two Basic Sections

Squares Divided into Two Basic Triangles
Squares Divided into Two Basic Rectangles

Patterns 570 to 617
Patterns 618 to 620

570. Birds in Air

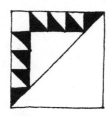

573. Star of Hope

571. Birds in the Air*

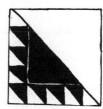

574. Sawtooth

572. Birds in the Air

575. Lend and Borrow†

* *Also:* Flying Geese.
† *Also:* Sawtooth.

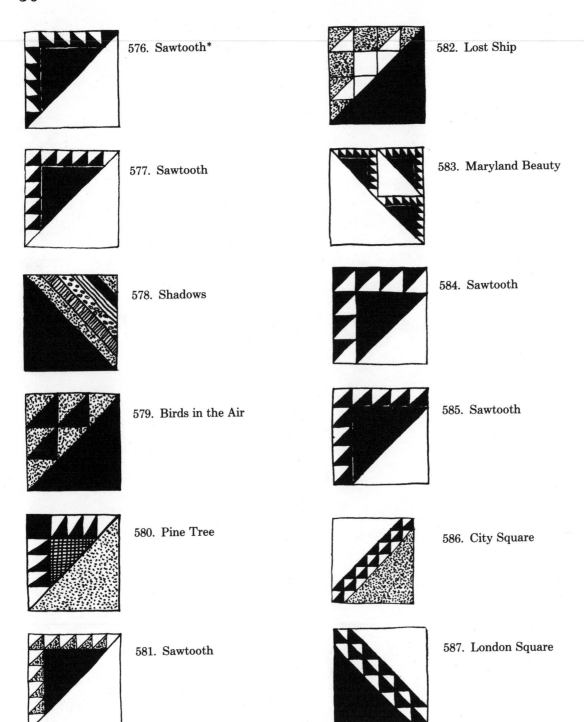

576. Sawtooth*

577. Sawtooth

578. Shadows

579. Birds in the Air

580. Pine Tree

581. Sawtooth

582. Lost Ship

583. Maryland Beauty

584. Sawtooth

585. Sawtooth

586. City Square

587. London Square

* *Also:* Kansas Trouble.

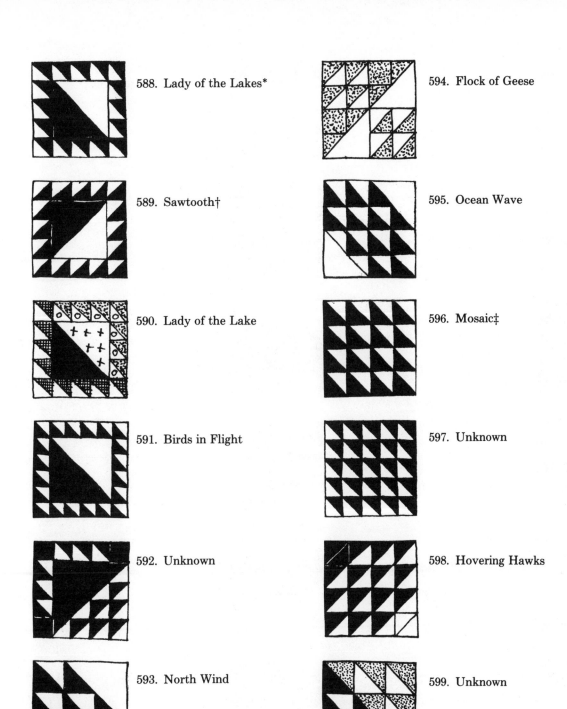

588. Lady of the Lakes*

589. Sawtooth†

590. Lady of the Lake

591. Birds in Flight

592. Unknown

593. North Wind

594. Flock of Geese

595. Ocean Wave

596. Mosaic‡

597. Unknown

598. Hovering Hawks

599. Unknown

* *Also:* Lady of the Lake.
† *Also:* Lady of the Lakes.
‡ *Also:* Geese in Flight.

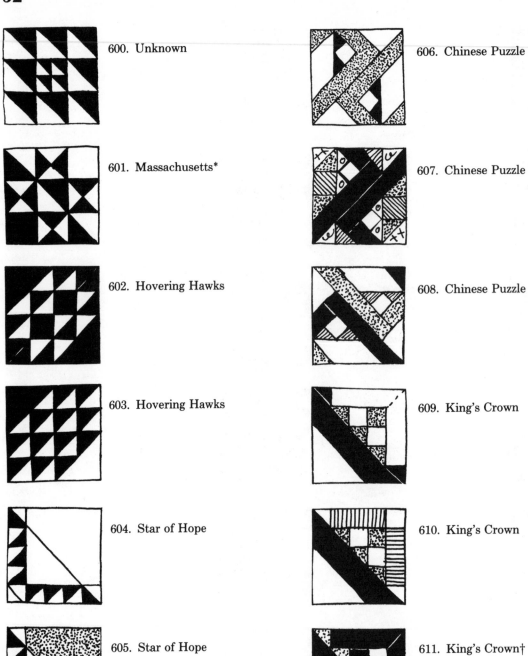

600. Unknown

601. Massachusetts*

602. Hovering Hawks

603. Hovering Hawks

604. Star of Hope

605. Star of Hope

606. Chinese Puzzle

607. Chinese Puzzle

608. Chinese Puzzle

609. King's Crown

610. King's Crown

611. King's Crown†

* *Also:* Cross and Crown.
† *Also:* Greek Cross.

 612. King's Crown Block

 613. Trail of Tears

 614. Indian Trail

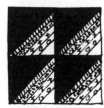 615. Amish Shadow Quilt (four blocks shown)

 616. Roman Stripes*

 617. Crazy Quilt

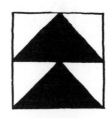 618. Wild Goose Chase

 619. Hill and Valley

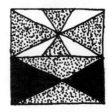 620. Whirlwind

* *Also:* Shadowed Squares.

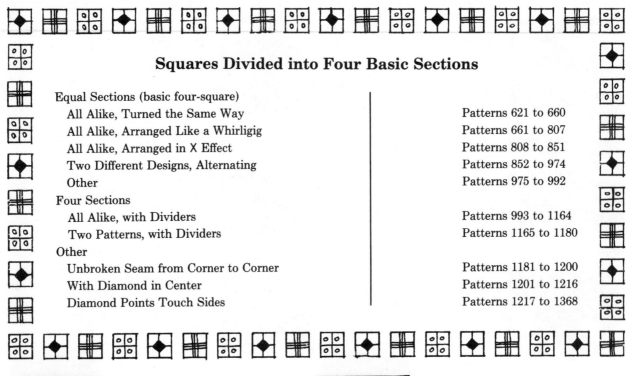

Squares Divided into Four Basic Sections

Equal Sections (basic four-square)
    All Alike, Turned the Same Way   Patterns 621 to 660
    All Alike, Arranged Like a Whirligig   Patterns 661 to 807
    All Alike, Arranged in X Effect   Patterns 808 to 851
    Two Different Designs, Alternating   Patterns 852 to 974
    Other   Patterns 975 to 992
Four Sections
    All Alike, with Dividers   Patterns 993 to 1164
    Two Patterns, with Dividers   Patterns 1165 to 1180
Other
    Unbroken Seam from Corner to Corner   Patterns 1181 to 1200
    With Diamond in Center   Patterns 1201 to 1216
    Diamond Points Touch Sides   Patterns 1217 to 1368

621. Compass

622. Unknown

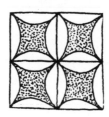

623. Trey's Quilt*

624. Unknown

625. Glorified Nine-patch

626. Snowball

* *Also:* Robbing Peter to Pay Paul.

 627. An Odd Pattern

 633. Lend and Borrow

 628. Unknown

 634. Flock of Geese

 629. Lost Ship

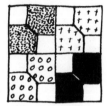 635. Tunnel Quilt*

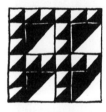 630. Lost Ship

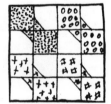 636. Joseph's Necktie

 631. Birds in the Air

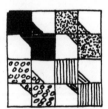 637. Joseph's Necktie

 632. Birds in Flight

 638. True Lover's Knot

* *Also:* Bow Tie.

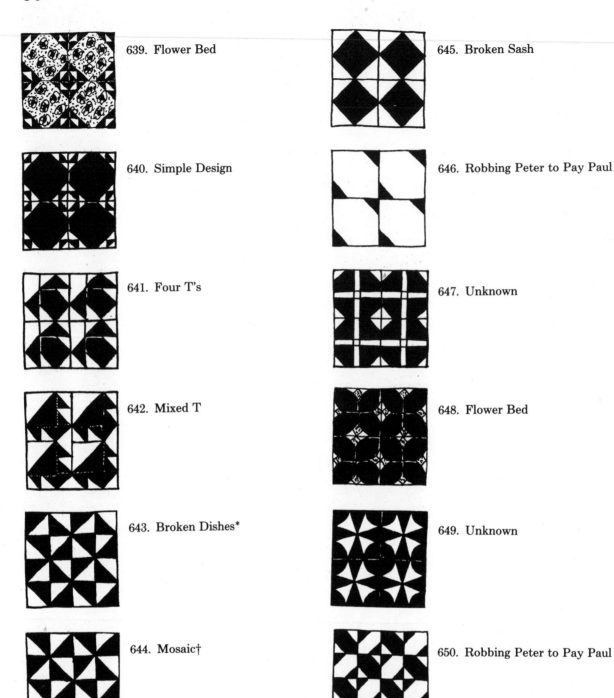

639. Flower Bed

640. Simple Design

641. Four T's

642. Mixed T

643. Broken Dishes*

644. Mosaic†

645. Broken Sash

646. Robbing Peter to Pay Paul

647. Unknown

648. Flower Bed

649. Unknown

650. Robbing Peter to Pay Paul

* *Also:* Birds in Air.
† *Also:* Windmill.

651. Devil's Claws

652. Attic Window

653. Edna's Pinwheel

654. Doodle-a-Quilt

655. Unknown

656. Kansas Dugout

657. King's Cross

658. Hatchet

659. Indian Hatchet

660. World's Fair

661. Old Crow*

662. Windmill†

* *Also:* Sugar Bowl, Fly, Kathy's Ramble, Crow's-foot, Fan Mill, Pinwheel.
† *Also:* Waterwheel, Millwheel, Pinwheel.

663. The Hourglass*

664. Big Dipper†

665. Pinwheel

666. Yankee Puzzle

667. Turnstyle

668. Whirlwind‡

669. Windmill

670. Broken Pinwheel

671. Windmill

672. Unknown

673. Windmill§

674. Flying Pinwheel

* *Also:* Windmill.
† *Also:* Envelope Quilt, Yankee Puzzle, Hourglass.
‡ *Also:* Pinwheel, Windmill.
§ *Also:* Whirligig, Turnstyle.

675. Windmill

676. Windblown Square

677. Windblown Square

678. Unknown-Four-patch

679. Dutchman's Puzzle

680. Dutchman's Puzzle

681. Mosaic

682. Swastika*

683. Swastika

684. Fly Foot

685. Windmill

686. Yankee Puzzle

* *Also:* Fly Foot, Devil's Puzzle.

687. Anna's Choice Quilt

688. Yankee Puzzle

689. Annie's Choice*

690. Mosaic

691. Mosaic†

692. Windmill

693. Windmill

694. Unknown

695. Eternal Triangle‡

696. Merry-Go-Round

697. Merry-Go-Round

698. Indian Trails§

* *Also:* Anna's Choice.
† *Also:* Barbara Frietchie Star.
‡ *Also:* Merry-Go-Round.
§ *Also:* Forest Path, Rambling Roads, Rambling Rose, Climbing Rose, North Wind, Irish Puzzle, Winding Walk, Old Maid's Ramble, Storm at Sea, Weathervane, Flying Dutchman, Prickly Pear, Tangled Tares, Bear's Paw.

699. Waves of the Sea

700. Kansas Trouble*

701. Kansas Trouble

702. Indian Trail

703. Kansas Trouble

704. Kansas Troubles

705. Kansas Trouble

706. Grand Right and Left

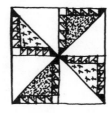

707. Indian Trails

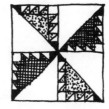

708. Indian Trails

709. Rolling Pinwheel

710. Whirling Pinwheel

* *Also:* Irish Puzzle.

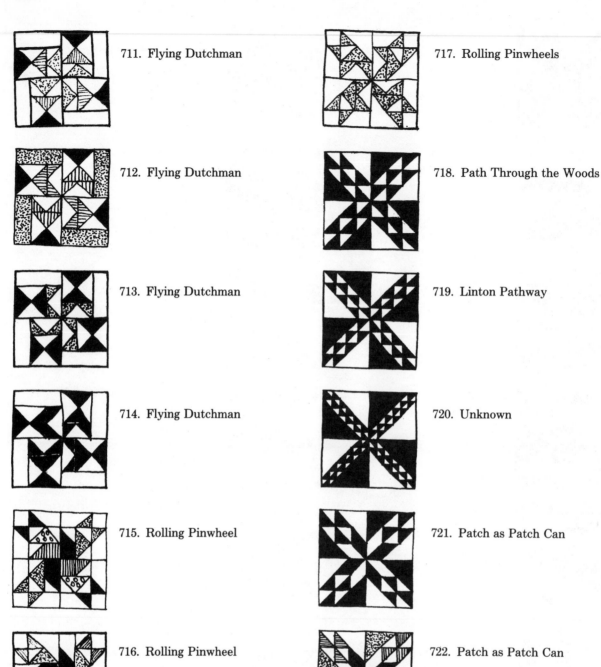

711. Flying Dutchman

712. Flying Dutchman

713. Flying Dutchman

714. Flying Dutchman

715. Rolling Pinwheel

716. Rolling Pinwheel

717. Rolling Pinwheels

718. Path Through the Woods

719. Linton Pathway

720. Unknown

721. Patch as Patch Can

722. Patch as Patch Can

 723. Log Cabin

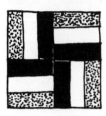 724. Roman Stripe

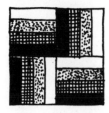 725. Propeller

 726. Roman Stripe

 727. Sewing Circle

 728. Arkansas Traveler

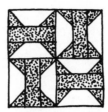 729. Arkansas Traveler

 730. Arkansas Traveler

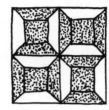 731. Spools

 732. Unknown

 733. Pinwheel

 734. Flying Saucer

735. Wheel of Fortune

741. Lady of the White House

736. Carnival Time

742. Nelson's Victory

737. Wheels

743. Nelson's Victory

738. Double Pinwheel

744. Windmill

739. Double Pinwheel

745. Seesaw

740. X Quartet

746. Windmill

 747. Louisiana

 753. Double Pinwheel

 748. End of Day

 754. Unknown

 749. Nelson's Victory

 755. Swastika

 750. Windmill

 756. Whirligig*

 751. Unknown

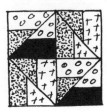 757. Turnabout Variation

 752. Double Pinwheel

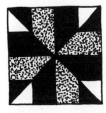 758. Turnabout Variation

* *Also:* Fly Foot, Devil's Puzzle.

759. Pinwheel

760. Pinwheel

761. Seesaw

762. Seesaw

763. T Quilt

764. Four E Block

765. Four Z Patch

766. Shooting Star

767. Clay's Choice

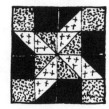

768. Clay's Choice

769. Variable Star

770. Taking Wing

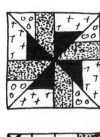 771. Turnabout Variation

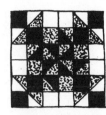 777. Square within Squares

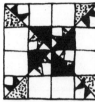 772. Unknown

 778. Greek Square

 773. Mrs. Morgan's Choice

 779. End of Day

 774. Night and Day

 780. Flying Fish

 775. Gretchen

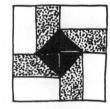 781. Susannah

 776. Squire Smith's Choice

 782. Whirling Star

783. A Scrap Zigzag

784. Holly Leaves

785. Dutch Windmill

786. The Ballet

787. American Flag

788. Unknown

789. Time and Energy

790. Bachelor's Puzzle

791. Springtime Blossoms

792. Square and Compass*

793. Alphabet Block

794. Idaho

* *Also:* Fore and Aft.

 795. Hearts and Gizzards*

 801. Mill Wheel†

 796. Twist and Turn

 802. Hunter's Star

 797. Unknown

 803. Unknown

 798. Springtime Blossoms

 804. Hearts and Gizzards

 799. Sunshine and Stained Glass

 805. Old Maid Combination

 800. Square and Compass

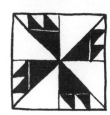 806. Rosebud

* *Also:* Wheel of Fortune.
† *Also:* Springtime Blossoms.

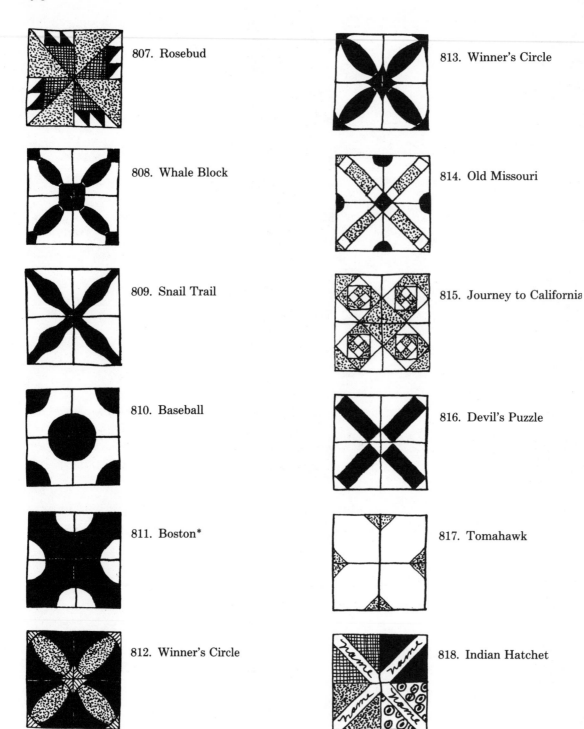

807. Rosebud

813. Winner's Circle

808. Whale Block

814. Old Missouri

809. Snail Trail

815. Journey to California

810. Baseball

816. Devil's Puzzle

811. Boston*

817. Tomahawk

812. Winner's Circle

818. Indian Hatchet

* *Also:* Boston Puzzle, Baseball.

819. Around the Farm

820. "I Do" Block

821. Unknown

822. Double Four-patch

823. Triangle

824. Mosaic

825. Bow Tie

826. True Lover's Knot

827. Magic Circle

828. Pullman Puzzle

829. Hearts and Gizzards

830. Orange Peel Reel

831. Bird of Paradise

832. Boston Puzzle

833. Alice's Tulips

834. Spiderweb*

835. Mother and Father Star

836. Union Square

837. Double X

838. Lisa's Choice

839. The Bridle Path

840. Butterfly Quadrille

841. Star Gardener

842. Unknown

* *Also:* String Quilt.

843. Rivoli Cross

849. Posy Patch

844. Amethyst Quilt

850. Galaxy

845. Pennsylvania

851. Mexican Rose

846. Arizona

852. Alternating Checkerboard

847. New Deal

853. Four-patch*

848. Square Deal

854. Autumn Tints

* *Also:* Double Four-patch.

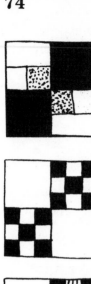

855. Tam's Patch

861. Borrow and Return

856. Single Irish Chain

862. Flashing Windmills

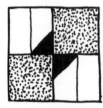

857. Unknown

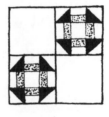

863. Sherman's March to the Sea

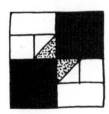

858. Necktie

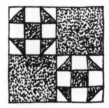

864. Unknown

859. Necktie

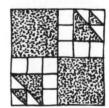

865. Unknown

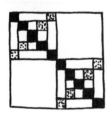

860. Country Lanes

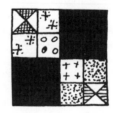

866. Unknown

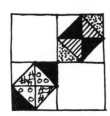 867. Bow Tie

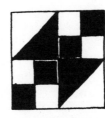 873. Northern Star

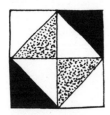 868. Broken Dishes

 874. Crosses and Losses

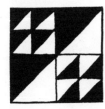 869. Flock of Geese

 875. Crosses and Losses

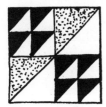 870. Flock

 876. Anvil

 871. Flock of Geese

 877. Crosses and Losses

 872. Jacob's Ladder

 878. Hollis Star

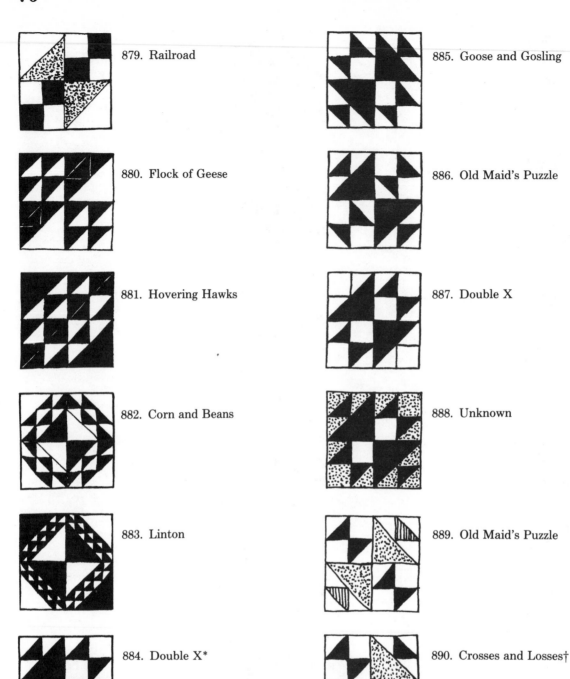

879. Railroad

880. Flock of Geese

881. Hovering Hawks

882. Corn and Beans

883. Linton

884. Double X*

885. Goose and Gosling

886. Old Maid's Puzzle

887. Double X

888. Unknown

889. Old Maid's Puzzle

890. Crosses and Losses†

* *Also:* Bow Tie, Old Maid's Puzzle, Fox and Geese, Crosses and Losses.
† *Also:* X, Double X, Old Maid's Puzzle.

 891. Crosses and Losses

 897. Alice Hegy's Double Four-patch

 892. Hovering Hawks*

 898. Old Maid's Puzzle†

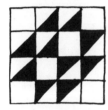 893. Anvil

 899. Dutchman's Puzzle

 894. Unknown

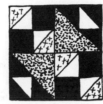 900. Unknown

 895. Ladies' Wreath

 901. Unknown

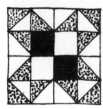 896. Chisholm Trail

 902. Battle of the Alamo

* *Also:* Hovering Birds.
† *Also:* Double X.

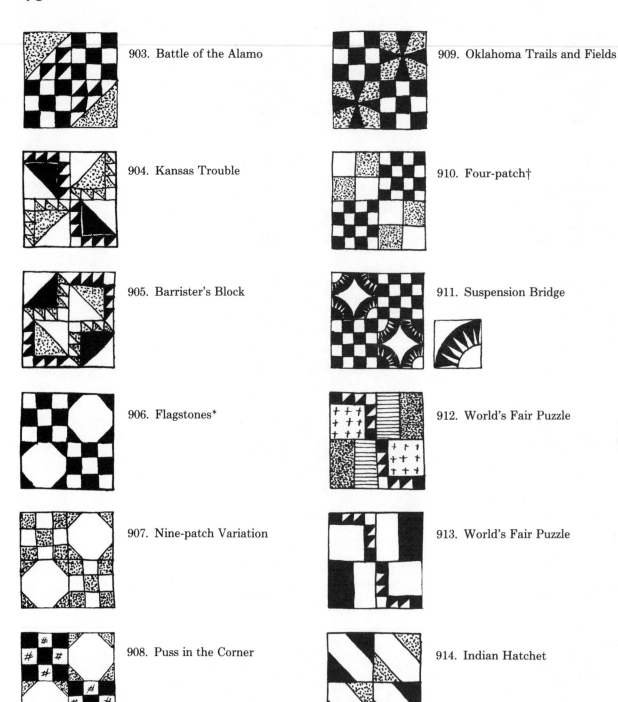

903. Battle of the Alamo

904. Kansas Trouble

905. Barrister's Block

906. Flagstones*

907. Nine-patch Variation

908. Puss in the Corner

909. Oklahoma Trails and Fields

910. Four-patch†

911. Suspension Bridge

912. World's Fair Puzzle

913. World's Fair Puzzle

914. Indian Hatchet

* *Also:* Snowball, The Snowball and Nine-patch.
† *Also:* Double Four-patch.

 915. Indian Hatchet

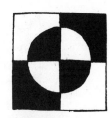 921. Rob Peter to Pay Paul‡

 916. Orange Peel Quilt

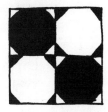 922. Robbing Peter to Pay Paul§

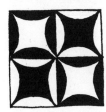 917. Robbing Peter to Pay Paul*

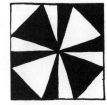 923. Shoemaker's Puzzle‖

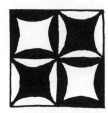 918. Dolly Madison's Workbox

 924. Robbing Peter to Pay Paul

 919. Rose Dream†

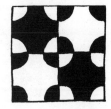 925. Mill Wheel

 920. Rose of Summer

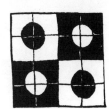 926. Polka Dot

* *Also:* Rob Peter to Pay Paul, Rob Peter and Pay Paul.
† *Also:* True Lover's Knot.
‡ *Also:* Snowball, Indiana Puzzle.
§ *Also:* Octagons, Hourglasses, Rob Peter to Pay Paul, Melon Patch.
‖ *Also:* Connecticut.

927. Electric Fans*

928. Light and Shadows

929. Melon Patch†

930. Compass

931. Melon Patch

932. Unknown

933. World without End

934. Unknown

935. Oklahoma

936. Four-square Variation

937. East and West‡

938. Hayes Corner

* *Also:* Grandma's Red and White Quilt.
† *Also:* Lafayette's Orange Peel.
‡ *Also:* The Broken Stone.

 939. Flying Clouds

 945. Double Tulip

 940. Eight-point Allover

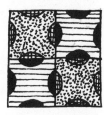 946. Dolly Madison's Work-basket

 941. Double Tifaifai

 947. Cross-patch

 942. Wedding Quilt

 948. Kentucky Chain

 943. Unknown

 949. Orange Squeezer

 944. Patience Corner

 950. Carolina Favorite

 951. Bow Tie

 957. Snowbound

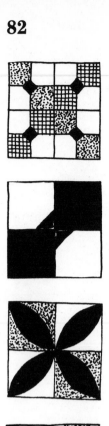 952. Necktie

 958. Small Business

953. Orange Peel

 959. Oklahoma Dogwood

 954. Old Mill Wheel

 960. V Block

 955. Flags and Ships

961. Whispering Leaves

 956. Next-door Neighbor

 962. Daisy Fan Quilt

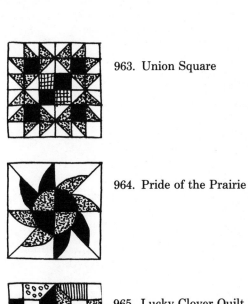 963. Union Square

 969. Hayes Corner

964. Pride of the Prairie

 970. Domino

 965. Lucky Clover Quilt

 971. Roman Stripe*

 966. Unknown

 972. Virginia Reel

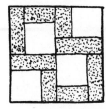 967. Patience Corner

 973. Chain and Hourglass

 968. Hayes' Corner

 974. Arrowhead Puzzle

* *Also:* Zigzag.

975. Barrister's Block

976. Lawyer's Puzzle

977. Barrister's Block

978. Windmill*

979. Corn and Beans

980. Unknown

981. Unknown

982. Sunny Lanes

983. Hourglass

984. A Victory Quilt

985. Stormy Sea

986. Ribbons

* *Also:* Corn and Peas, Hourglass.

987. Unknown

988. Flutterby

989. Aircraft*

990. Flower Garden Path

991. Necktie

992. Necktie

993. Road to California

994. Unknown

995. Blackford's Beauty

996. Fanny's Favorite

997. West Virginia

998. Army Star

* *Also:* Airplane.

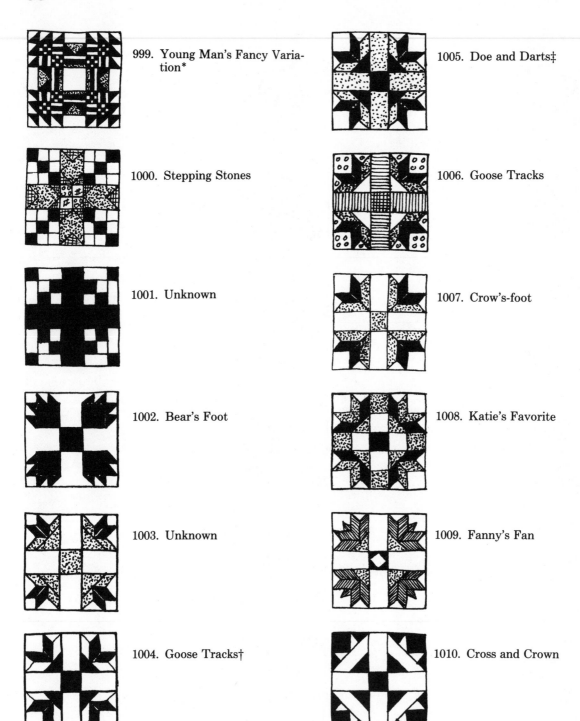

999. Young Man's Fancy Variation*

1000. Stepping Stones

1001. Unknown

1002. Bear's Foot

1003. Unknown

1004. Goose Tracks†

1005. Doe and Darts‡

1006. Goose Tracks

1007. Crow's-foot

1008. Katie's Favorite

1009. Fanny's Fan

1010. Cross and Crown

* *Also:* Nebraska.
† *Also:* Fancy Flowers, Duck's Foot in the Mud, Bear's Paw.
‡ *Also:* David and Goliath, Four Darts, Bulls-eye, Flying Darts.

1011. Mexican Star*

1012. Goose Tracks†

1013. Fannie's Fan

1014. David and Goliath

1015. Mexican Star

1016. Mexican Star

1017. David and Goliath‡

1018. Signal

1019. Cross and Crown

1020. Cross and Crown

1021. Cross and Crown

1022. Fanny's Fan

* *Also:* Mexican Cross.
† *Also:* Duck Paddle, Cross and Crown.
‡ *Also:* Four Darts, Bull's-eye, Flying Darts, Doe and Darts.

1023. Fannie's Fan

1029. Jack-in-the-Box

1024. Bear's Paw

1030. Jack-in-the-Box

1025. Bull's-eye

1031. Jack-in-the-Box

1026. Bachelor's Puzzle

1032. Bird's Nest

1027. Bachelor's Puzzle

1033. Bird's Nest

1028. Bachelor's Puzzle

1034. Bird's Nest

1035. Pinwheel Square

1036. Crazy Ann

1037. Pinwheel Square

1038. Unknown

1039. Minnesota

1040. Propeller

1041. Crazy House

1042. Presentation Quilt

1043. Unknown

1044. Honey's Choice

1045. Honey's Choice

1046. Premium Star

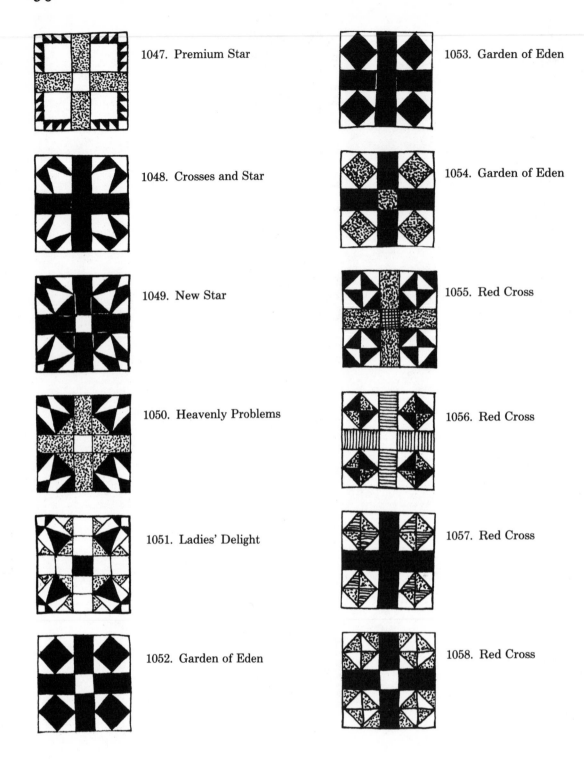

1047. Premium Star

1048. Crosses and Star

1049. New Star

1050. Heavenly Problems

1051. Ladies' Delight

1052. Garden of Eden

1053. Garden of Eden

1054. Garden of Eden

1055. Red Cross

1056. Red Cross

1057. Red Cross

1058. Red Cross

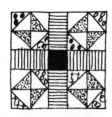 1059. Red Cross

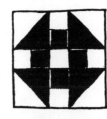 1065. Aeroplane*

 1060. Plaid

 1066. Double Wrench

 1061. Churn Dash

 1067. Alaska Homestead

 1062. Five-patch Star

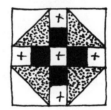 1068. Double Wrench

 1063. Four X Star

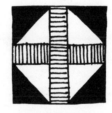 1069. Unknown

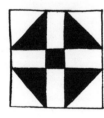 1064. Shoofly

 1070. Grandmother's Choice

* *Also:* Wrench.

1071. Cross and Crown

1077. Duck and Ducklings

1072. Duck and Ducklings

1078. Handy Andy†

1073. Corn and Beans*

1079. Handy Andy

1074. Duck and Ducklings

1080. Unknown

1075. Unknown

1081. Flying Geese

1076. Duck and Ducklings

1082. Handy Andy

* *Also:* Duck and Ducklings, Hen and Chickens, Wild Goose Chase, Grandmother's Choice, Handy Andy.
† *Also:* Flying Geese.

 1083. The White Square Quilt

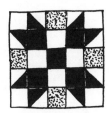 1089. Sister's Choice

 1084. Mare's Nest

 1090. Inverted T

 1085. Wedding Ring

 1091. Unknown

 1086. T Blocks

 1092. Wild Rose and Square

 1087. Unknown

 1093. Joseph's Coat

 1088. Georgia

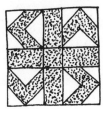 1094. Farmer's Puzzle

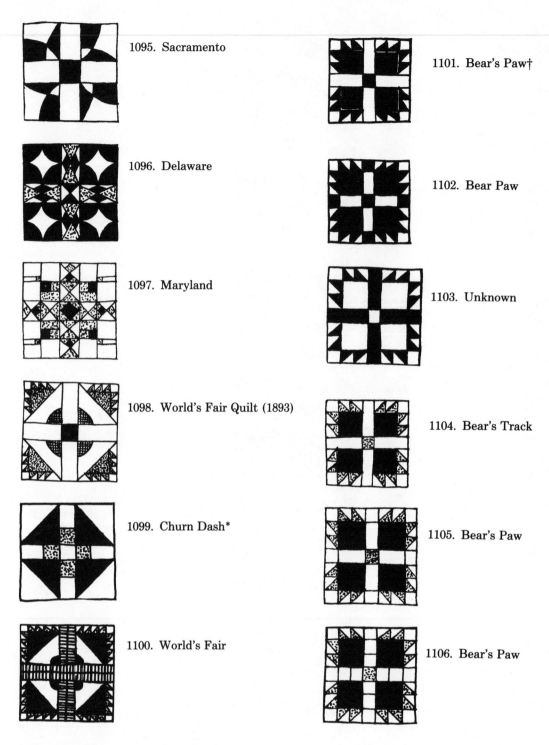

1095. Sacramento

1096. Delaware

1097. Maryland

1098. World's Fair Quilt (1893)

1099. Churn Dash*

1100. World's Fair

1101. Bear's Paw†

1102. Bear Paw

1103. Unknown

1104. Bear's Track

1105. Bear's Paw

1106. Bear's Paw

* *Also:* Lovers' Knot, Monkey Wrench.
† *Also:* Duck's Foot in the Mud, Lily Design, Hand of Friendship, Cross and Crown, Goose Tracks, Bear's Foot, Bear's Claw, Quaker Handshake, Illinois Turkey Track.

 1107. Bear's Paw

 1113. Hen and Chickens

 1108. Bear's Paw

 1114. Dove in the Window

 1109. Unknown

 1115. Hen and Chickens

 1110. Autumn Tints

 1116. Dove in the Window

 1111. Dove in the Window

 1117. Rosebud

 1112. Hen and Chickens

 1118. The Question Block

1119. Stonemason's Puzzle

1120. Lincoln's Platform

1121. Lincoln's Platform

1122. Lincoln's Platform

1123. Lincoln's Platform

1124. Lincoln's Platform

1125. Lincoln's Platform

1126. Lincoln's Platform

1127. Nine-patch

1128. Lincoln's Platform

1129. Abe Lincoln's Platform

1130. Cross and Crown

 1131. David and Goliath

 1137. Mayflower

 1132. Dove at the Window

 1138. Unknown

 1133. Fannie's Fan

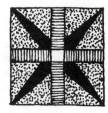 1139. King David's Crown

 1134. David and Goliath

 1140. Windowpane

 1135. Bear's Paw

 1141. Prickly Pear

 1136. Country Roads

 1142. Premium Star

 1143. Premium Star

 1149. Cross and Crown

 1144. Bear's Den

 1150. Goose Tracks

 1145. Turkey Tracks

 1151. Variable Star

 1146. Turkey Tracks

 1152. Flying Geese

 1147. Turkey Tracks

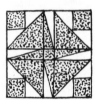 1153. Crazy Ann

 1148. Unknown

 1154. Windmill

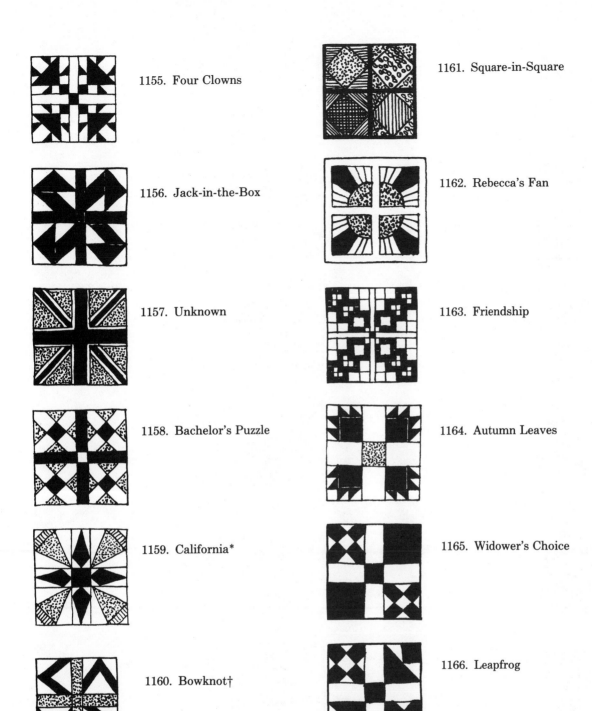

1155. Four Clowns

1156. Jack-in-the-Box

1157. Unknown

1158. Bachelor's Puzzle

1159. California*

1160. Bowknot†

1161. Square-in-Square

1162. Rebecca's Fan

1163. Friendship

1164. Autumn Leaves

1165. Widower's Choice

1166. Leapfrog

* *Also:* Snowflake.
† *Also:* Farmer's Puzzle.

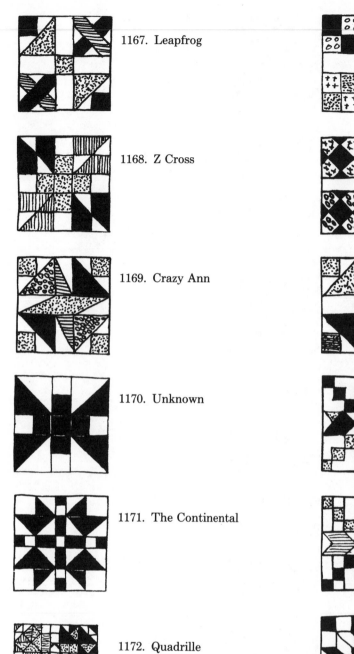

1167. Leapfrog

1168. Z Cross

1169. Crazy Ann

1170. Unknown

1171. The Continental

1172. Quadrille

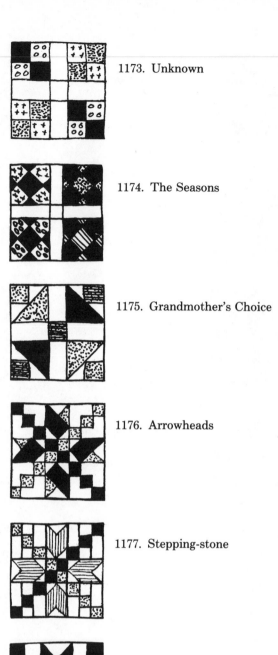

1173. Unknown

1174. The Seasons

1175. Grandmother's Choice

1176. Arrowheads

1177. Stepping-stone

1178. Merry Kite

 1179. Blackford's Beauty*

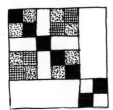 1180. Cross in the Square

 1181. Twin Sisters

 1182. Whirlwind

 1183. Windmill†

 1184. Windmill

 1185. Crazy Ann

 1186. String Quilt

 1187. Unknown

 1188. Crazy Pieces

 1189. Jeffrey's Nine-patch

 1190. Bride's Prize (pieced and appliquéd)

* *Also:* Good Cheer.
† *Also:* Waterwheel, Mill Wheel.

1191. Sarah's Favorite

1197. Granny's Choice

1192. Old Maid's Ramble

1198. Unknown

1193. Old Maid's Ramble (reverse alternating blocks)

1199. Unknown

1194. Boise

1200. The Range's Pride

1195. Granny's Choice

1201. Susannah

1196. Spools

1202. Susannah

 1203. Susannah Patch

 1209. Windblown Square

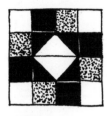 1204. Susannah

 1210. Bachelor's Puzzle

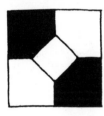 1205. Amish Bow Tie

 1211. Bachelor's Puzzle

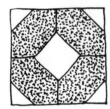 1206. Kansas Dugout

 1212. Irish Puzzle.

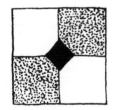 1207. Necktie

 1213. Cheyenne

 1208. Mosaic

 1214. Cheyenne

104

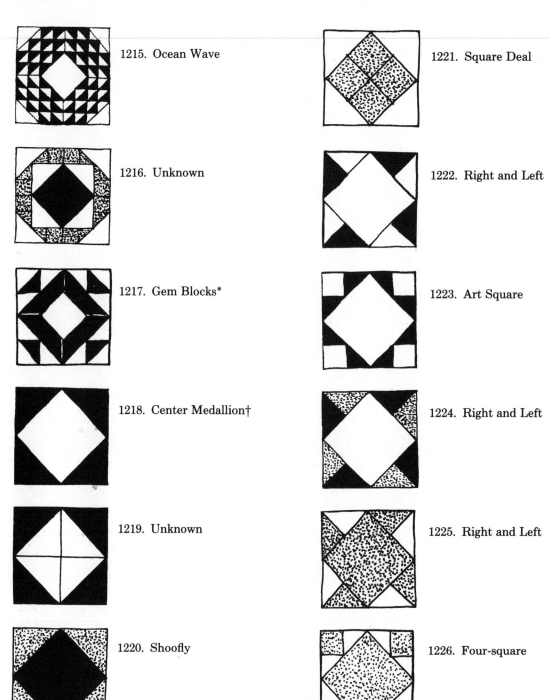

1215. Ocean Wave

1216. Unknown

1217. Gem Blocks*

1218. Center Medallion†

1219. Unknown

1220. Shoofly

1221. Square Deal

1222. Right and Left

1223. Art Square

1224. Right and Left

1225. Right and Left

1226. Four-square

* *Also:* Mosaic.
† *Also:* Square in Square, Shoofly.

 1227. Cracker

 1228. Broken Dishes

 1229. Snail Trail

 1230. Unknown

 1231. Unknown

 1232. End of the Road

 1233. The Broken Path

 1234. Snail Trail

 1235. Unknown

 1236. Unknown

 1237. A Design for Patriotism

 1238. Country Checkers

 1239. Corn and Beans

 1245. Puss in the Corner

1240. Puss in the Corner*

 1246. Aunt Sukey's Choice

1241. Aunt Sukey's Choice

 1247. Aunt Sukey's Choice

 1242. Aunt Sukey's Choice

 1248. Unknown

1243. Aunt Sukey's Choice

 1249. Christmas Star

 1244. Puss in Corner

 1250. Royal Star

* *Also:* Puss in Boots.

 1251. The Arrowhead Star

 1257. Weathervane

 1252. Many-pointed Star

 1258. Unknown

 1253. Weathervane

 1259. Unknown

 1254. Weathervane

 1260. Interlocked Square

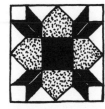 1255. Unknown

 1261. Unknown

 1256. The Cornerstone

 1262. Interlaced Squares

 1263. Squares in Squares

 1269. Unknown

 1264. Twelve Triangles

 1270. Storm Signal

 1265. Twenty-four Triangles

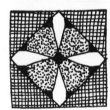 1271. Unknown

 1266. Unknown

 1272. Star

 1267. Coffin Star

 1273. Maltese Cross

 1268. Coffin Star

 1274. The Airplanes

 1275. Unknown

 1281. Floral Bouquet

 1276. Star of Bethlehem

 1282. Economy

 1277. Letter H

 1283. Road to Paris

 1278. Maltese Cross

 1284. Mosaic

 1279. Maltese Cross

 1285. Double Squares*

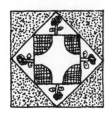 1280. Spiced Pinks

 1286. Broken Dishes

* *Also:* Jack-in-the-Pulpit, Broken Dishes, Double Square.

1287. Jack-in-the-Pulpit

1288. Jack-in-the-Pulpit

1289. Double Squares

1290. Mosaic

1291. Unknown

1292. Unknown

1293. Unknown

1294. Unknown

1295. Grandpa's Favorite

1296. Windblown Square*

1297. Unknown

1298. Windblown Square†

* *Also:* Balkan Puzzle, Zigzag Tile.
† *Also:* Balkan Puzzle.

1299. Unknown

1305. Georgetown Circles

1300. Unknown

1306. Crown of Thorns*

1301. Unknown

1307. Crazy Ann

1302. Georgetown Circles

1308. Crazy Ann

1303. Square and Star

1309. Crazy Ann

1304. Georgetown Circle

1310. Crazy Ann

* *Also:* Georgetown Circle, Memory Wreath.

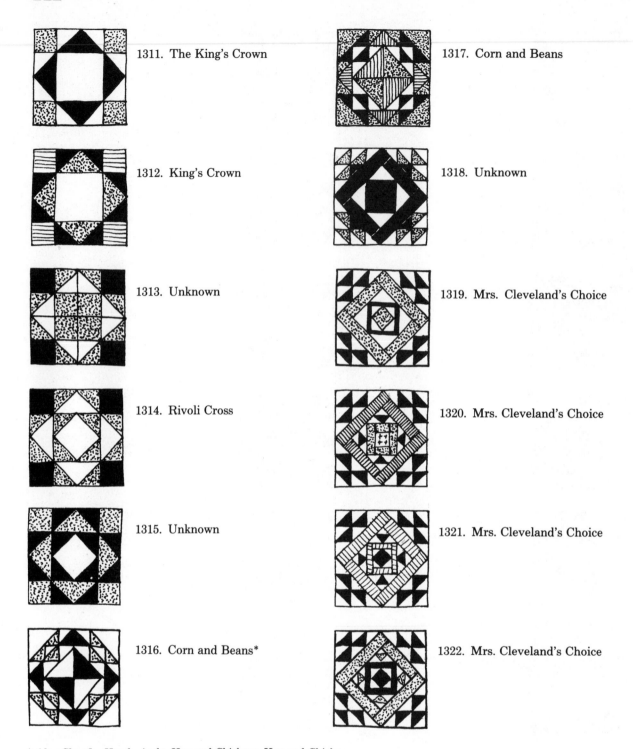

1311. The King's Crown

1317. Corn and Beans

1312. King's Crown

1318. Unknown

1313. Unknown

1319. Mrs. Cleveland's Choice

1314. Rivoli Cross

1320. Mrs. Cleveland's Choice

1315. Unknown

1321. Mrs. Cleveland's Choice

1316. Corn and Beans*

1322. Mrs. Cleveland's Choice

* *Also:* Shoofly, Handy Andy, Hen and Chickens, Hen and Chicks.

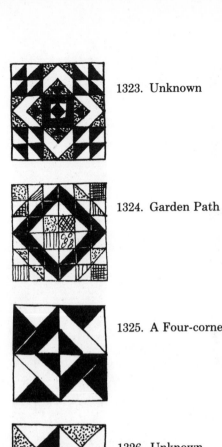 1323. Unknown

 1329. Cross within a Cross

1324. Garden Path

 1330. Cross within Cross

 1325. A Four-corner Puzzle

 1331. Unknown

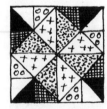 1326. Unknown

 1332. Unknown

1327. Unknown

 1333. Unknown

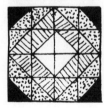 1328. Quilter's Surprise

 1334. Pine Burr

1335. Unknown

1336. Unknown

1337. Iowa

1338. The Square Deal

1339. Broken Window

1340. Unknown

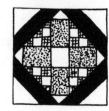

1341. Unknown

1342. Mosaic

1343. Mosaic

1344. Four Points

1345. King's Crown

1346. Mosaic

 1347. Mosaic

 1353. Unknown

 1348. Mosaic

 1354. Unknown

 1349. Morning Patch

 1355. Crosses within Squares*

 1350. Nine-patch Star

 1356. Ladyfinger and Sunflower

 1351. The Road to Oklahoma

 1357. Fort Sumter

 1352. Unknown

 1358. Fern Pattern

* *Also:* Cabin Windows.

1359. Indiana

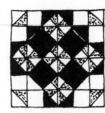

1365. South Dakota

1360. Stars and Stirrups

1366. Frankfort

1361. Strawberry*

1367. Indiana Puzzle

1362. Swallows in the Window

1368. Grandmother's Choice

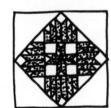

1363. Delectable Mountains

1364. Lansing

* *Also:* Full-blown Tulip, Oriental Star.

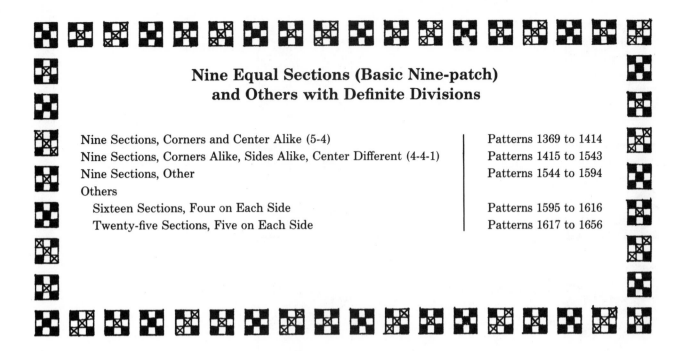

Nine Equal Sections (Basic Nine-patch)
and Others with Definite Divisions

Nine Sections, Corners and Center Alike (5-4)	Patterns 1369 to 1414
Nine Sections, Corners Alike, Sides Alike, Center Different (4-4-1)	Patterns 1415 to 1543
Nine Sections, Other	Patterns 1544 to 1594
Others	
Sixteen Sections, Four on Each Side	Patterns 1595 to 1616
Twenty-five Sections, Five on Each Side	Patterns 1617 to 1656

1369. Checkerboard

1372. Bow Tie*

1370. Flag In, Flag Out

1373. Road to California

1371. Crisscross

1374. Jacob's Ladder

* *Also:* Lover's Knot.

117

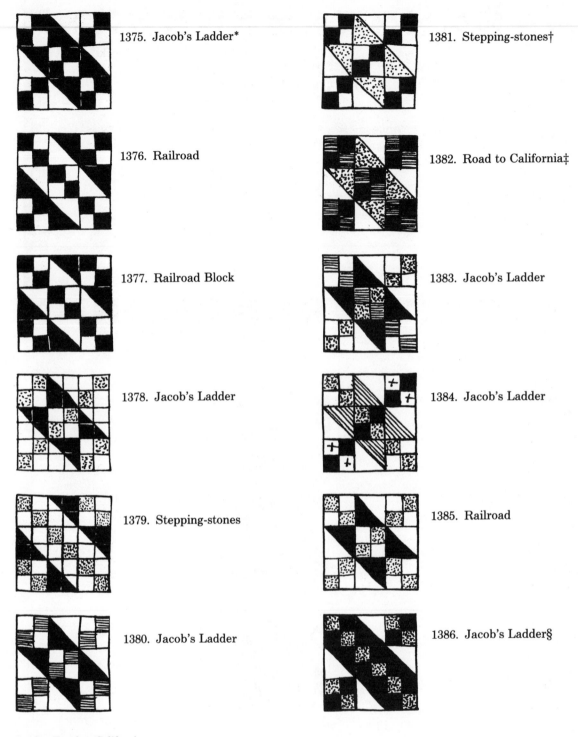

1375. Jacob's Ladder*

1376. Railroad

1377. Railroad Block

1378. Jacob's Ladder

1379. Stepping-stones

1380. Jacob's Ladder

1381. Stepping-stones†

1382. Road to California‡

1383. Jacob's Ladder

1384. Jacob's Ladder

1385. Railroad

1386. Jacob's Ladder§

* *Also:* Road to California.
†*Also:* Tail of Benjamin's Kite, Underground Railroad, Trail of the Covered Wagons, Wagon Tracks, Rocky
  Road to California, Jacob's Ladder, Rocky Road to Oklahoma.
‡ *Also:* Jacob's Ladder.
§ *Also:* Road to California.

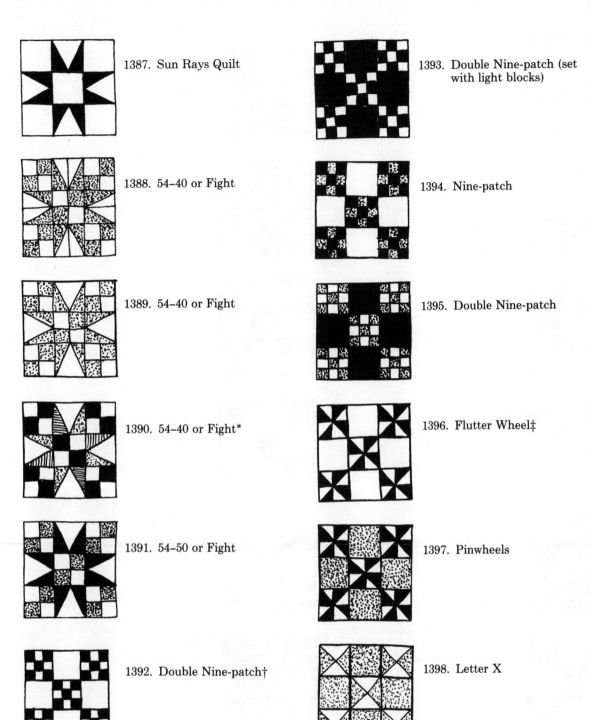

1387. Sun Rays Quilt

1388. 54–40 or Fight

1389. 54–40 or Fight

1390. 54–40 or Fight*

1391. 54–50 or Fight

1392. Double Nine-patch†

1393. Double Nine-patch (set with light blocks)

1394. Nine-patch

1395. Double Nine-patch

1396. Flutter Wheel‡

1397. Pinwheels

1398. Letter X

* *Also:* Meteor.
† *Also:* Baby Nine-patch, Puss in the Corner.
‡ *Also:* Pinwheel.

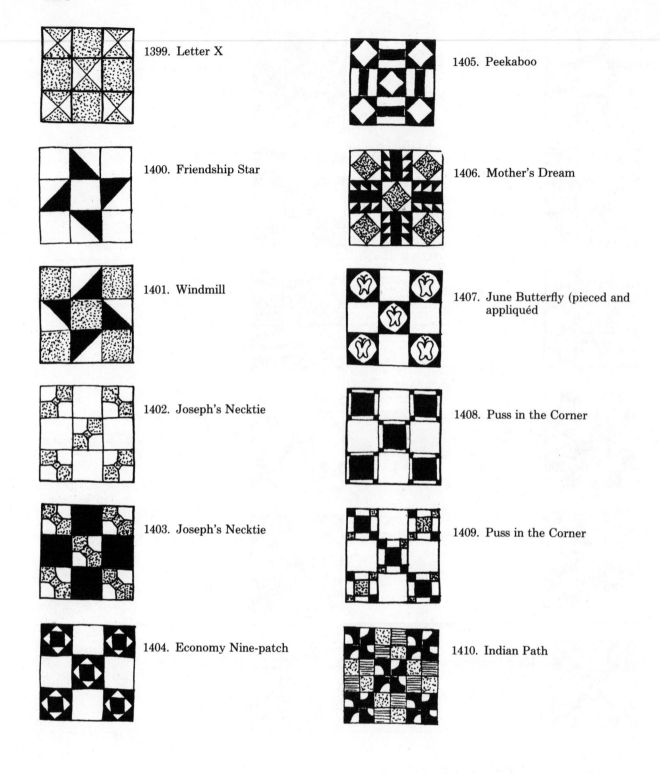

1399. Letter X

1405. Peekaboo

1400. Friendship Star

1406. Mother's Dream

1401. Windmill

1407. June Butterfly (pieced and appliquéd

1402. Joseph's Necktie

1408. Puss in the Corner

1403. Joseph's Necktie

1409. Puss in the Corner

1404. Economy Nine-patch

1410. Indian Path

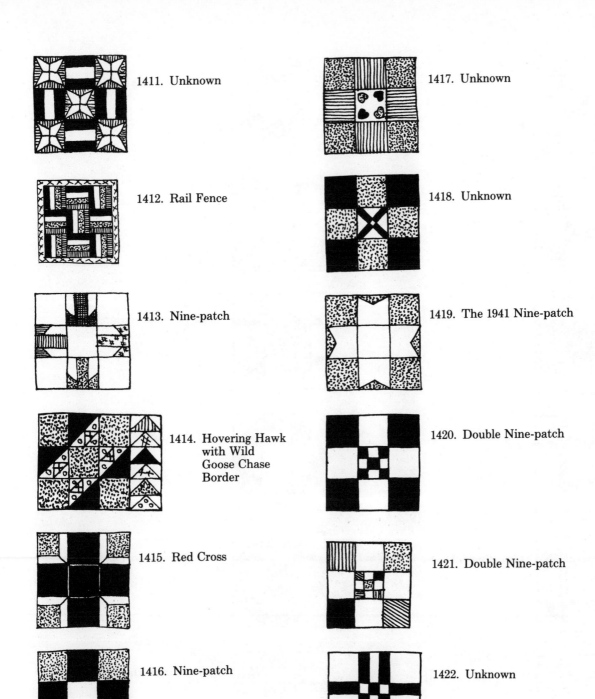

1411. Unknown

1412. Rail Fence

1413. Nine-patch

1414. Hovering Hawk
with Wild
Goose Chase
Border

1415. Red Cross

1416. Nine-patch

1417. Unknown

1418. Unknown

1419. The 1941 Nine-patch

1420. Double Nine-patch

1421. Double Nine-patch

1422. Unknown

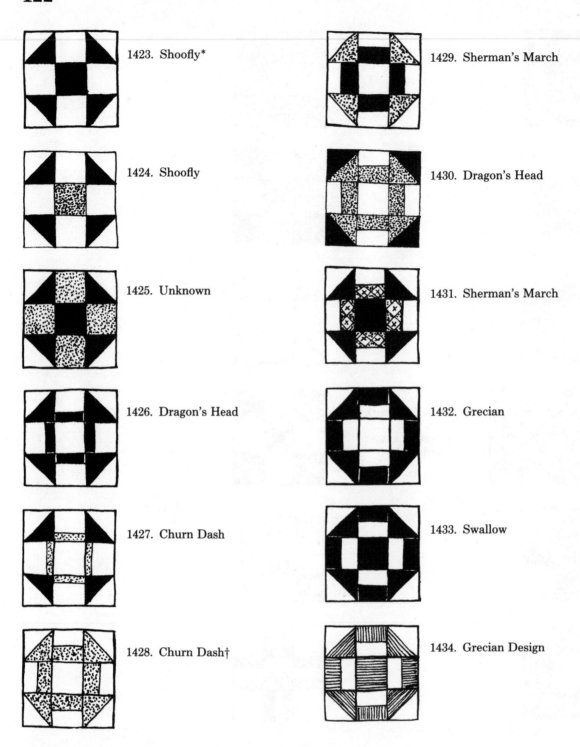

1423. Shoofly*

1424. Shoofly

1425. Unknown

1426. Dragon's Head

1427. Churn Dash

1428. Churn Dash†

1429. Sherman's March

1430. Dragon's Head

1431. Sherman's March

1432. Grecian

1433. Swallow

1434. Grecian Design

* *Also:* Fence Row, Shoofly.
† *Also:* Hole in the Barn Door, Monkey Wrench, Double Monkey Wrench, Sherman's March, Barn Door, Chinese Coin, Shoofly, Broken Plate, Crow's Nest, Love Knot, Lincoln's Platform, Pioneer Block, Pioneer Patch, Picture Frame, Quail's Nest, Indian Hammer.

 1435. Creek Cross

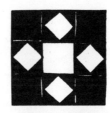 1441. Unknown

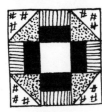 1436. Double Monkey Wrench

 1442. Sawtooth Patchwork

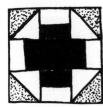 1437. Creek Cross

 1443. Sawtooth Patchwork

 1438. Mosaic

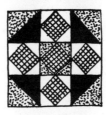 1444. Unknown

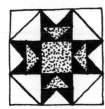 1439. Capital T

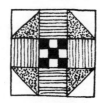 1445. Unknown

 1440. Capital T

 1446. Golden Gate*

* *Also:* Puss in the Corner.

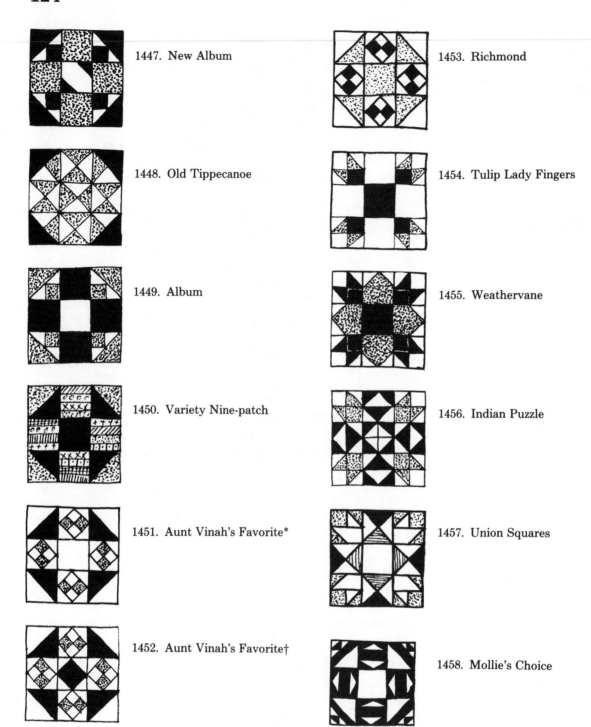

1447. New Album

1448. Old Tippecanoe

1449. Album

1450. Variety Nine-patch

1451. Aunt Vinah's Favorite*

1452. Aunt Vinah's Favorite†

1453. Richmond

1454. Tulip Lady Fingers

1455. Weathervane

1456. Indian Puzzle

1457. Union Squares

1458. Mollie's Choice

* *Also:* Butterfly, Richmond, VA.
† *Also:* Butterfly, Richmond, VA, Cross and Chains.

1459. Girl's Joy

1460. Crisscross

1461. Tail of Benjamin's Kite

1462. Unknown

1463. Tangled Garter*

1464. Rolling Stones

1465. Puss in the Corner

1466. Rolling Stone

1467. Rolling Stone

1468. Combination Star

1469. Combination Star

1470. Montpelier

* *Also:* Garden Maze, Sundial, Tirzah's Treasure.

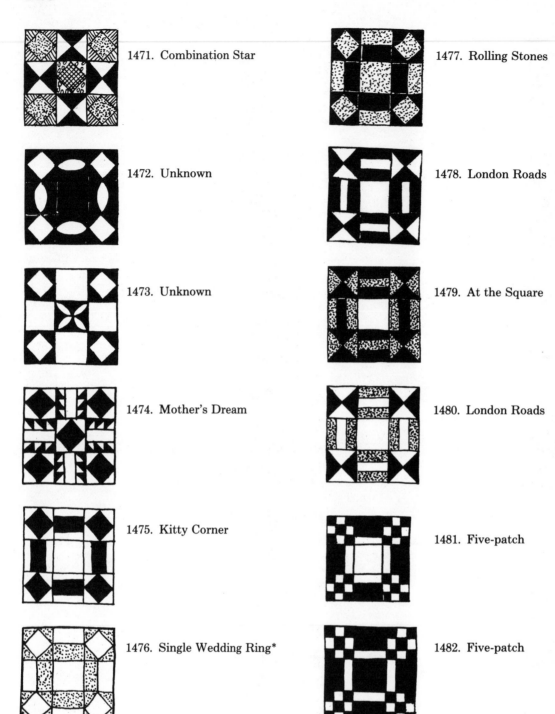

1471. Combination Star

1472. Unknown

1473. Unknown

1474. Mother's Dream

1475. Kitty Corner

1476. Single Wedding Ring*

1477. Rolling Stones

1478. London Roads

1479. At the Square

1480. London Roads

1481. Five-patch

1482. Five-patch

* *Also:* Wheel.

 1483. Puss in the Corner

 1489. Double T

 1484. Texas Star

 1490. Illinois

 1485. Silent Star

 1491. Double T

 1486. Snowflake

 1492. Unknown

 1487. Morning Star

 1493. T Block

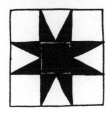 1488. Unknown

 1494. Turkey Tracks

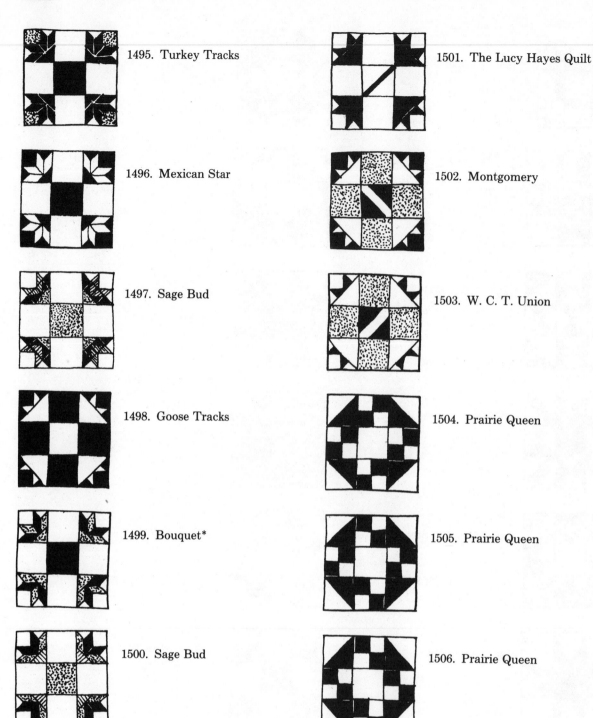

1495. Turkey Tracks

1496. Mexican Star

1497. Sage Bud

1498. Goose Tracks

1499. Bouquet*

1500. Sage Bud

1501. The Lucy Hayes Quilt

1502. Montgomery

1503. W. C. T. Union

1504. Prairie Queen

1505. Prairie Queen

1506. Prairie Queen

* *Also:* Sage Bud.

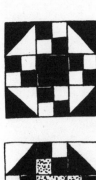 1507. Unknown

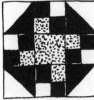 1508. Prairie Queen

 1509. Prairie Queen

 1510. Pinwheels

 1511. Chapel Window

 1512. Sunlight and Shadows

 1513. Butterflies and Blossoms

 1514. Spirit of '71.

 1515. Chicago Star

 1516. Chicago Star

 1517. Chicago Star

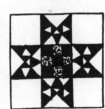 1518. Dolly Madison Star

 1519. Joseph's Coat

 1525. Arrow Point

 1520. Unknown

 1526. Unknown

1521. King David's Crown

 1527. Joseph's Coat

1522. The Practical Orchard

 1528. Independence Square

1523. Letter X

 1529. Morning Star

 1524. Santa Fe Block

 1530. Unknown

 1531. Queen's Crown

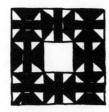 1537. Beggar Block

 1532. Salem

 1538. Beggar's Block

 1533. Tulip Garden

 1539. Beggar Block

 1534. Bluebell

 1540. Beggar Block

 1535. Hand Weave

 1541. Unknown

 1536. Garden Maze

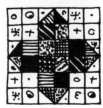 1542. Cathedral Squares

 1543. Unknown

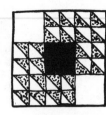 1549. Winged Square

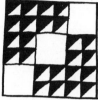 1544. Cut-glass Dish

 1550. Double X

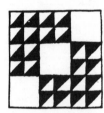 1545. Winged Square

 1551. The Harrison Quilt

 1546. Cut-glass Dish

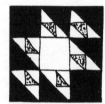 1552. Cat's Cradle

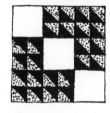 1547. Winged Square

 1553. The Cat's Cradle

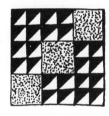 1548. Cut-glass Dish

 1554. Flying Bird

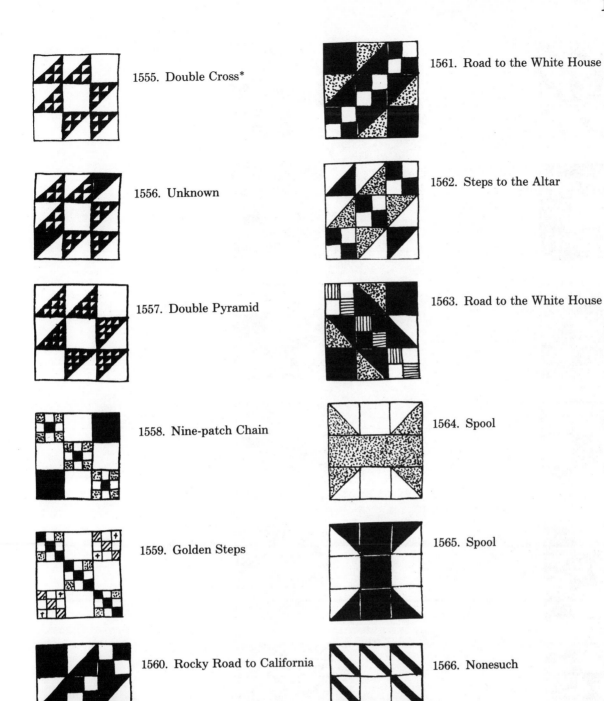

1555. Double Cross*

1556. Unknown

1557. Double Pyramid

1558. Nine-patch Chain

1559. Golden Steps

1560. Rocky Road to California

1561. Road to the White House

1562. Steps to the Altar

1563. Road to the White House

1564. Spool

1565. Spool

1566. Nonesuch

* *Also:* Pyramid, Double Pyramids.

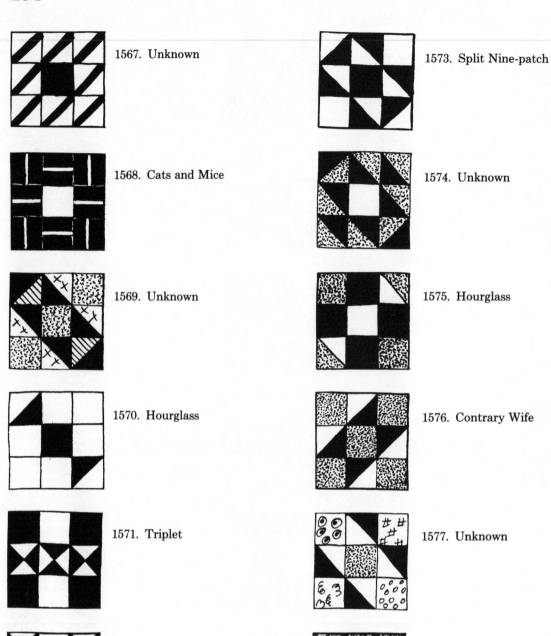

1567. Unknown

1573. Split Nine-patch

1568. Cats and Mice

1574. Unknown

1569. Unknown

1575. Hourglass

1570. Hourglass

1576. Contrary Wife

1571. Triplet

1577. Unknown

1572. Unknown

1578. Salad Bowl

 1579. Indian Arrowheads

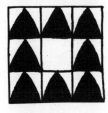 1580. Bells of Ireland

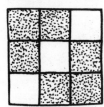 1581. Patience

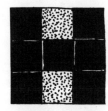 1582. Pennsylvania Dutch Hex Sign

 1583. Waterwheel

 1584. Waterwheel

 1585. Waterwheel

 1586. Bird of Paradise

 1587. Indiana Puzzle

 1588. Eight-pointed Star

 1589. The Broken Circle

 1590. Mississippi

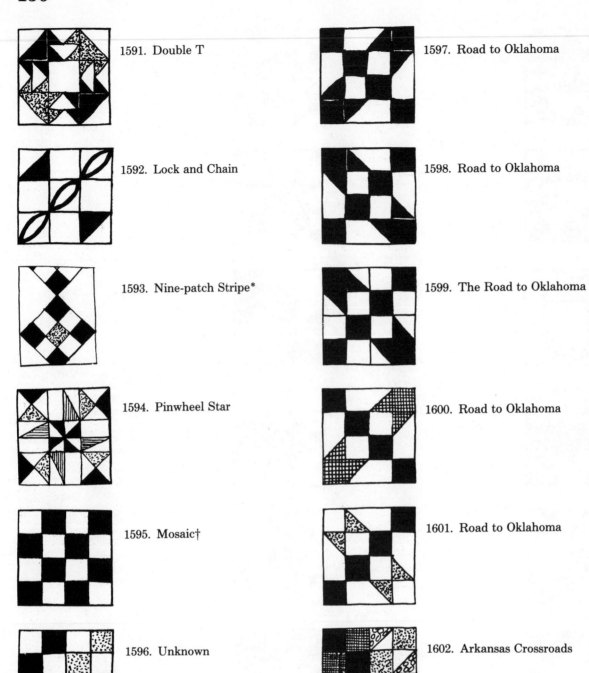

1591. Double T

1592. Lock and Chain

1593. Nine-patch Stripe*

1594. Pinwheel Star

1595. Mosaic†

1596. Unknown

1597. Road to Oklahoma

1598. Road to Oklahoma

1599. The Road to Oklahoma

1600. Road to Oklahoma

1601. Road to Oklahoma

1602. Arkansas Crossroads

* *Also:* Tipped-over Nine-patch.
† *Also:* Nine-patch.

1603. Shoofly

1609. Pinwheel

1604. Orange Peel*

1610. Pinwheel

1605. Yankee Puzzle

1611. Streak of Lightning

1606. Illusion Block

1612. Unknown

1607. Nelson's Victory

1613. Indiana Puzzle†

1608. Pinwheel

1614. World's Fair Block

* *Also:* Reel.
† *Also:* Chinese Coin, Monkey Wrench.

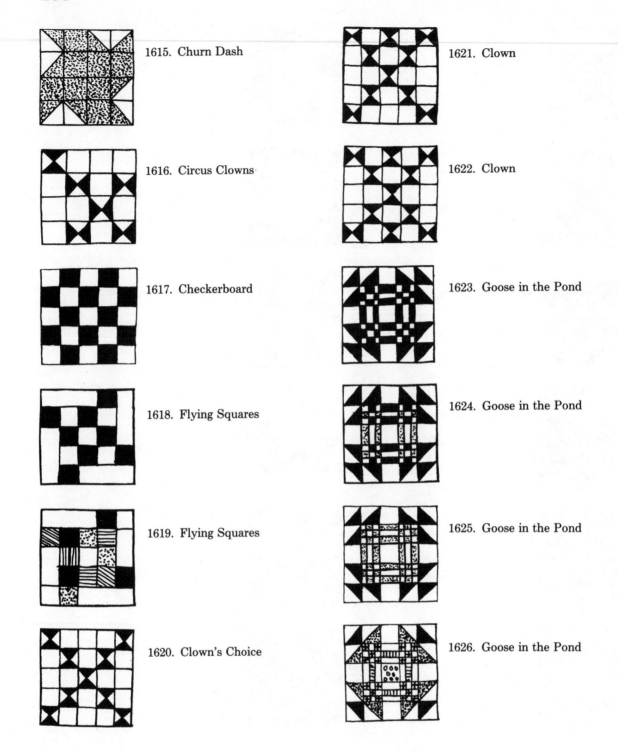

1615. Churn Dash

1616. Circus Clowns

1617. Checkerboard

1618. Flying Squares

1619. Flying Squares

1620. Clown's Choice

1621. Clown

1622. Clown

1623. Goose in the Pond

1624. Goose in the Pond

1625. Goose in the Pond

1626. Goose in the Pond

 1627. Missouri Puzzle

 1633. Old Scraps Patchwork

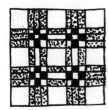 1628. Album Patch

 1634. Wishing Ring

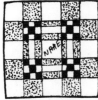 1629. Album Quilt

 1635. Georgetown Circle

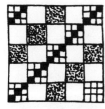 1630. Nine-patch Chain

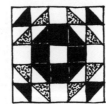 1636. Unknown

 1631. Country Lanes

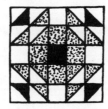 1637. Unknown

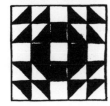 1632. Wedding Ring

 1638. Wedding Ring

1639. Handy Andy

1640. Album

1641. Handy Andy

1642. Handy Andy

1643. Wedding Rings

1644. Star and Cross

1645. Sister's Choice

1646. Sister's Choice

1647. Nine-patch Star

1648. Four-X Star

1649. Four-X Star

1650. Sister's Choice

 1651. Sister's Choice

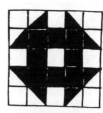 1654. Chinese Coin

 1652. Unknown

 1655. Philadelphia Pavement

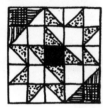 1653. Queen Charlotte's Crown

 1656. Pigeon Toes

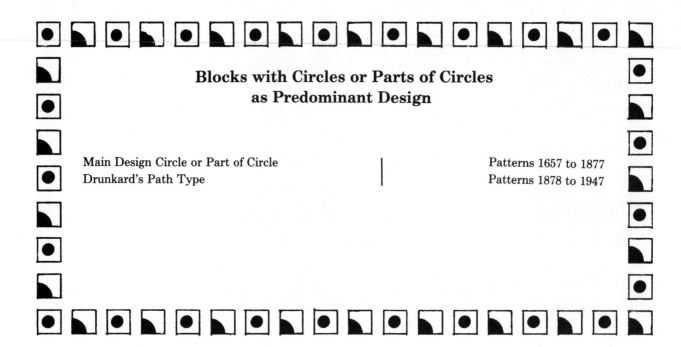

Blocks with Circles or Parts of Circles
as Predominant Design

Main Design Circle or Part of Circle   Patterns 1657 to 1877

Drunkard's Path Type   Patterns 1878 to 1947

1657. Baby Aster

1660. Dresden Plate

1658. Morning Glory

1661. Dresden Plate

1659. Baby Aster

1662. True Lover's Buggy Wheel*

* *Also:* Wheel of Chance.

1663. Dresden Plate

1669. Unknown

1664. Dresden Plate

1670. Dresden Plate

1665. Dresden Plate

1671. Dresden Plate* (number of wedges may vary)

1666. Chrysanthemum

1672. Dresden Plate

1667. Dresden Plate

1673. Dresden Plate

1668. Dresden Plate

1674. Dresden Plate

* *Also:* Lazy Daisy.

 1675. Dresden Plate

 1681. Fancy Dresden Plate

1676. Friendship Ring

 1682. Alcazar*

1677. Dresden Plate

 1683. Grecian Star

 1678. Dresden Plate (21 petals)

 1684. Dresden Plate

 1679. Dresden Plate

 1685. Dresden Plate

 1680. Dresden Plate

 1686. Dresden Plate

* *Also:* Full-blown Tulip, Young Man's Invention.

 1687. Dresden Plate

 1693. Sunflower

 1688. Sunflower

 1694. Dresden Plate Variation

 1689. Dresden Plate

 1695. Fancy Dresden Plate

 1690. Dresden Plate

 1696. Wedding Ring

 1691. Friendship Ring

 1697. Double Wedding Ring

 1692. Sunflower

1698. Double Wedding Ring

 1699. Double Wedding Ring

 1705. The Pickle Dish

 1700. Double Wedding Ring (when small, Baby Wedding Ring)

 1706. Job's Tears

 1701. Double Wedding Ring*

1707. The Star Chain

 1702. Golden Wedding Ring

 1708. Pyrotechnics

 1703. Three-corner Wedding Ring

 1709. Rainbow

1704. Indian Wedding Ring†

 1710. Unknown

* *Also:* Double Wedding Bands, Wedding Ring.
† *Also:* Pickle Dish.

 1711. Unknown

 1717. Single Sunflower

 1712. Sunflower

 1718. Sunflower

 1713. Unknown

 1719. A Brave Sunflower

 1714. Rising Sun* (pieced and appliquéd)

 1720. Sunflower Star

 1715. Rising Sun

 1721. Dahlia

 1716. Georgetown Circle

 1722. Pearl Buck Quilt (note 14 points)

* *Also:* Georgetown Circle.

148

 1723. Sunset

 1729. Simple Compass

 1724. Sawtooth Circle

 1730. Cog Wheels

 1725. Sunflower

 1731. Topeka

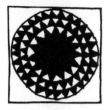 1726. Missouri Sunflower

 1732. Crown Variation

 1727. Friendship Frame (pieced and appliquéd)

 1733. Calico Compass

 1728. Full-blown Tulip

 1734. Calico Compass

 1735. Full-blown Tulip*

 1736. Full-blown Tulip

 1737. Caesar's Crown (pieced and appliquéd)

 1738. Rose Album

 1739. Caesar's Crown

 1740. Caesar's Crown

 1741. Dogwood

 1742. Victoria's Crown (pieced and appliquéd)

 1743. Pilot's Wheel

 1744. Strawberry

 1745. Strawberry

 1746. Pilot's Wheel

Also: Dutch Tulip.

 1747. The Strawberry

 1753. Joseph's Coat*

 1748. Strawberry (pieced and appliquéd)

 1754. Full-blown Tulip

 1749. Strawberry

 1755. The Strawberry

 1750. Pilot's Wheel

 1756. Whirlwind

 1751. Caesar's Crowns

 1757. Wheel of Time

 1752. Unknown

 1758. Wheel of Fortune

* *Also:* Traditional Pattern.

 1759. Suspension Bridge*

 1765. Whig Defeat‡

 1760. Suspension Bridge

 1766. Grandmother's Engagement Ring

 1761. Indian Summer

 1767. Whig's Defeat

 1762. Split Rail†

 1768. Lotus Blossom§

 1763. Baby Bunting

 1769. Grandmother's Engagement Ring

 1764. Fan

 1770. Fannie's Favorite

* *Also:* Sunburst, Broken Circle, Sunflower.
† *Also:* Indian Summer.
‡ *Also:* Grandmother's Engagement Ring.
§ *Also:* Richmond Beauty.

1771. Orange Peel

1772. Lafayette Orange Peel

1773. Flower Petals

1774. Orange Peel

1775. Unknown

1776. Unknown

1777. The Reel

1778. Tulip Wheel

1779. Unknown

1780. Melon Patch

1781. Robbing Peter to Pay Paul

1782. Trenton Quilt

 1783. Trenton

 1789. New Frontier

 1784. Lafayette Orange Peel

 1790. Wagon Wheels

 1785. Rob Peter to Pay Paul

 1791. Wheels

 1786. Bow Tie

 1792. Unknown

 1787. Tea Leaf

 1793. Wheel of Fortune

 1788. Wandering Foot*

 1794. True Lover's Buggy Wheel

* *Also:* Turkey Track.

 1795. Circle of Life

 1801. Drunkard's Path

 1796. Circle within Circle

 1802. Friendship Knot*

 1797. Circle within Circle

 1803. New Wedding Ring

 1798. Crossroads

 1804. Drunkard's Trail

 1799. Crossed Roads to Texas

 1805. The Rainbow Quilt

 1800. Crossroads

 1806. Oriole Window†

* *Also:* Starry Crown.
† *Also:* Circular Saw, Four Little Fans.

 1807. Circular Saw

 1813. Black-eyed Susan

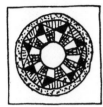 1808. Garden Spot

 1814. Glorified Nine-patch

 1809. Rhododendron Star

 1815. Unknown

 1810. Rhododendron Star

 1816. Improved Nine-patch*

 1811. Unknown

 1817. Milwaukee's Own

 1812. Evelyne's Whirling Dust Storm

 1818. Orange Peel

* *Also:* Bailey's Nine-patch.

 1819. Ferris Wheel

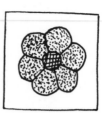 1825. Mother's Flower Garden
(pieced and appliquéd)

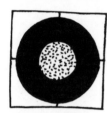 1820. Ferris Wheel

 1826. Crown

 1821. The Golden Wedding
Ring

 1827. Crown

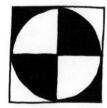 1822. Unknown

 1828. Hearts and Rings

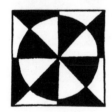 1823. Unknown

 1829. Bride's Quilt

 1824. Mother's Flower Garden
(pieced and appliquéd)

 1830. Wyoming Patch

 1831. Queen of the May

 1837. Unknown

 1832. Rainbow Star Quilt

 1838. Unknown

 1833. Odds and Ends

 1839. Fair Play

 1834. Fortune's Wheel

 1840. Unknown

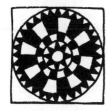 1835. Georgetown Circle*

 1841. Moon and Stars

 1836. Circles and Crosses

 1842. Snowball (white)†

* *Also:* Oklahoma Star, Rising Sun.
† *Also:* Fireball (red), Rising Sun.

 1843. Washington Merry-Go-Round

 1849. Pickle Dish

 1844. Utah

 1850. Bull's-eye

 1845. Mill Wheel

 1851. Sunburst

 1846. Merry-Go-Round

 1852. Hickory Leaf

 1847. Compass*

 1853. The Jinx Star

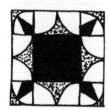 1848. Queen's Pride

 1854. Four-o'-clock Quilt

* *Also:* The Compass Quilt, Love Entanglement.

 1855. Grandmother's Brooch of Love

 1861. Unknown

 1856. Snowball Wreath

 1862. The Rolling Stone

 1857. Circular Saw

 1863. Unknown

 1858. Air Ship

 1864. Chinese Gongs

1865. Rainbow

 1859. Hero's Crown

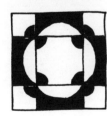 1860. Queen's Crown

 1866. Job's Tears

1867. Robbing Peter to Pay Paul

1873. Slave Chain

1868. Whig Rose

1874. Mother's Choice Quilt

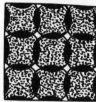

1869. My Graduation Class Ring

1875. Missouri Trouble

1870. Queen's Crown

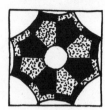

1876. Links of Friendship

1871. Queen's Crown

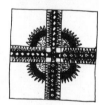

1877. Rocky Mountain Road

1872. Unknown

1878. Drunkard's Path*

* *Also:* Rocky Road to Dublin, Rocky Road to California, Country Husband.

 1879. Solomon's Puzzle*

 1885. Fool's Puzzle‡

 1880. Solomon's Puzzle

 1886. Wonder of the World§

 1881. World's Puzzle†

 1887. Fool's Puzzle

 1882. Drunkard's Path

 1888. Wonder of the World

 1883. Drunkard's Trail

 1889. Harvest Moon

 1884. Solomon's Puzzle

 1890. Fool's Puzzle

* *Also:* Rocky Road to California.
† *Also:* Solomon's Puzzle.
‡ *Also:* Wonder of the World.
§ *Also:* Tumbleweed.

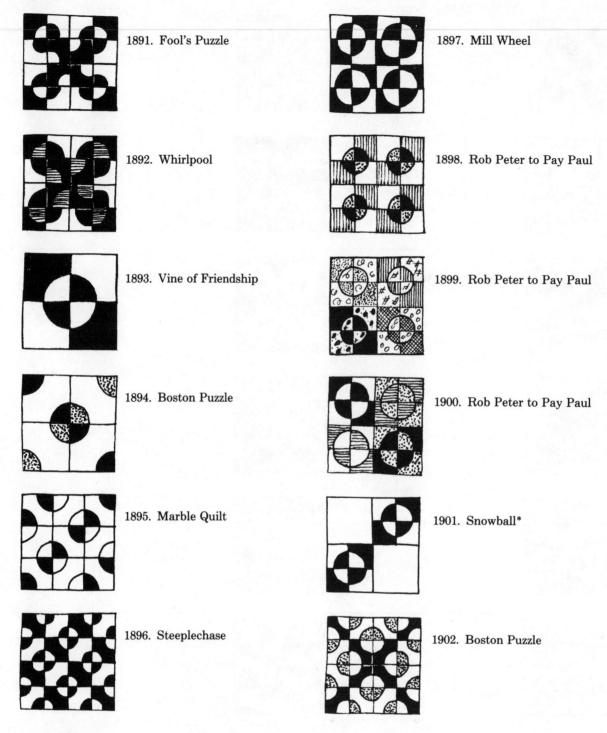

1891. Fool's Puzzle

1892. Whirlpool

1893. Vine of Friendship

1894. Boston Puzzle

1895. Marble Quilt

1896. Steeplechase

1897. Mill Wheel

1898. Rob Peter to Pay Paul

1899. Rob Peter to Pay Paul

1900. Rob Peter to Pay Paul

1901. Snowball*

1902. Boston Puzzle

* *Also:* Indiana Puzzle, Rob Peter to Pay Paul.

1903. Harvest Moon*

1904. Around the World

1905. Drunkard's Path Variation

1906. Unknown

1907. Sunshine and Shadows

1908. Drunkard's Path†

1909. Drunkard's Path

1910. Cleopatra's Puzzle

1911. Cleopatra's Puzzle

1912. Illinois Rose

1913. Mohawk Trail

1914. Baby Bunting

* *Also:* Around the World.
† *Also:* Rocky Road to Dublin, Rocky Road to California, Country Husband, Robbing Peter to Pay Paul.

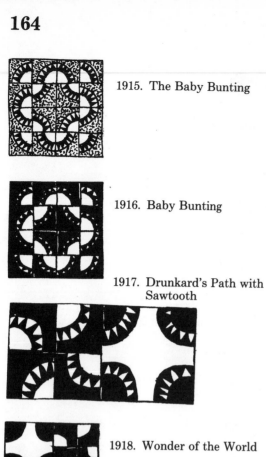

1915. The Baby Bunting

1916. Baby Bunting

1917. Drunkard's Path with Sawtooth

1918. Wonder of the World

1919. Drunkard's Trail

1920. Rippling Waters

1921. Falling Timbers

1922. Diagonal Stripes

1923. Vine of Friendship

1924. Unknown

1925. Vine of Friendship*

1926. Snake Trail

* *Also:* Dove, Falling Timbers, Snake Trail.

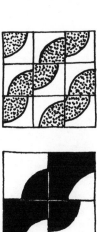 1927. Chain Quilt

 1933. Drunkard's Path

1928. Doves

 1934. Robbing Peter to Pay Paul

1929. The Dove

1935. Fool's Puzzle*

 1930. Mill Wheel

 1936. Drunkard's Path

1931. Drunkard's Path

 1937. Moorish Design

 1932. Mill Wheel

  1938. Drunkard's Garden

* *Also:* Wonder of the World, Country Husband.

 1939. Chainlinks

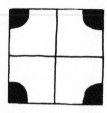 1944. Mill Wheel

 1940. Nonesuch*

 1945. Dirty Windows

 1941. Falling Timbers

  1946. West Virginia Lily

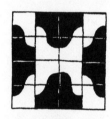 1942. Unknown

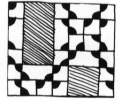 1947. Drunkard's Patchwork

 1943. Mushrooms

* *Also:* Love Ring, Sun Dance.

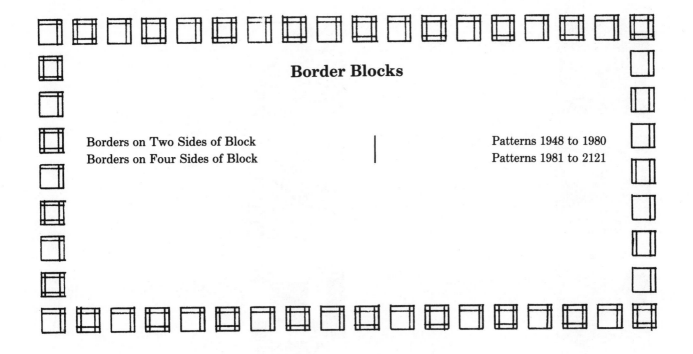

Border Blocks

Borders on Two Sides of Block
Borders on Four Sides of Block

Patterns 1948 to 1980
Patterns 1981 to 2121

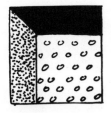 1948. Shadow Box

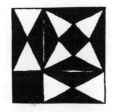 1951. Diamond and Star

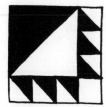 1949. Unknown

 1952. Diamond and Star

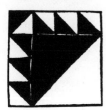 1950. Delectable Mountains

 1953. New York Beauty

1954. New York Beauty

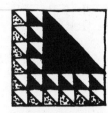

1960. Lost Ships

1955. Springtime in the Rockies

1961. Unknown

1956. Storm at Sea

1962. Children's Delight

1957. Unknown

1963. Nine-patch

1958. Queen's Favorite

1964. Children's Delight

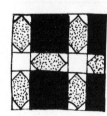

1959. Stars and Stripes

1965. Children's Delight

 1966. Unknown

 1972. Bouquet and Fan*

 1967. Children's Delight

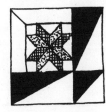 1973. Bouquet in a Fan

 1968. Dragonfly

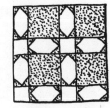 1974. Vestibule

 1969. Darting Minnow

 1975. Nine-patch

 1970. Happy Hunting Grounds

 1976. Storm at Sea

 1971. Pineapple

 1977. Milky Way

* *Also:* Nosegay.

1978. Road to California

 1984. Unknown

 1979. Grandma's Favorite

 1985. Philadelphia Pavement

 1980. Oregon

 1986. Hayes Corner

 1981. Unknown

 1987. Missouri Puzzle

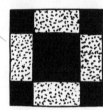 1982. Nine-patch

 1988. Eddystone Light

 1983. White House Steps

 1989. Aunt Eliza's Star

 1990. Unknown

 1991. New Album

 1992. Unknown

 1993. Coxey's Camp

 1994. Coxey's Camp

 1995. Philadelphia Pavement

 1996. Philadelphia Pavement

 1997. Philadelphia Pavement

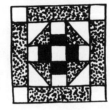 1998. The Crow's Nest

 1999. Monkey Wrench

 2000. Road to California

 2001. Unknown

 2002. A Little Girl's Star

 2008. Unknown

 2003. Unknown

 2009. Unknown

 2004. Robbing Peter to Pay Paul

 2010. Unknown

 2005. Union*

 2011. Prickly Pear

 2006. Union

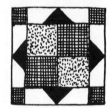 2012. Chain

 2007. Unknown

 2013. Rolling Pinwheel

* *Also:* Union Block.

 2014. Unknown

 2020. Chain

 2015. Georgetown Circle*

 2021. Zigzag

 2016. Friendship Quilt

 2022. Double Sawtooth

 2017. The Diamond Cross

 2023. Massachusetts

 2018. Indian Emblem Quilt

 2024. Indian Hatchet

 2019. Unknown

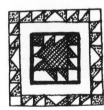 2025. Indian Hatchett

*Also: Crown of Thorns, Wedding Ring.

2026. Indian Plumes

2027. Flying Clouds*

2028. Flying Clouds

2029. Odds and Ends

2030. Unknown

2031. Unknown

2032. True Lover's Knot

2033. True Lover's Knot

2034. Missouri Puzzle

2035. Missouri Puzzle

2036. Ribbon Square

2037. Mother's Fancy

* *Also:* Four Frogs.

 2038. Puss in the Corner

 2044. Square and a Half

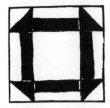 2039. Churn Dash

 2045. Double X

 2040. Triangles and Stripes

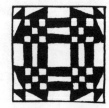 2046. Spider's Den

 2041. Unknown

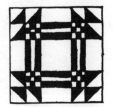 2047. Unknown

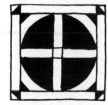 2042. Unknown

 2048. Unknown

 2043. Grandmother's Favorite

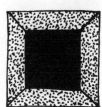 2049. The Diversion Quilt

176

 2050. Unknown

 2056. Square and Circle

 2051. Hourglass

 2057. Unknown (pieced and embroidered flowers)

 2052. King's Crown

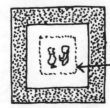 2058. White House Steps

 2053. Frame a Print

 2059. Mosaic

 2054. Unknown

 2060. Unknown

 2055. Unknown

 2061. Unknown

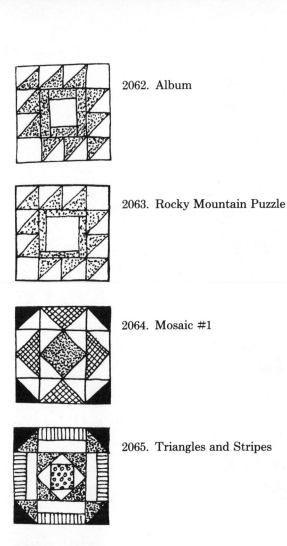

2062. Album

2063. Rocky Mountain Puzzle

2064. Mosaic #1

2065. Triangles and Stripes

2066. Tulip*

2067. Free Trade Patch

2068. Framed Cross

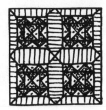

2069. Framed Cross

2070. Four-leaf Clover

2071. Four-leaf Clover

2072. Grandmother's Cross

2073. Shepherd's Crossing†

* *Also:* Lady Finger.
† *Also:* Grandmother's Own.

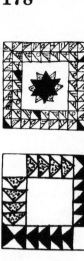 2074. Double Star (pieced and appliquéd)

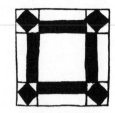 2080. Johnnie*

 2075. Wild Goose Chase

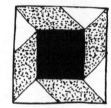 2081. Box Quilt Pattern

 2076. Wild Goose Chase

 2082. Box†

 2077. Storm at Sea

 2083. Box Quilt

 2078. Storm at Sea

 2084. Formal Garden

 2079. Storm at Sea

 2085. Contrary Husband

* *Also:* Around the Corner.
† *Also:* Open Box, Eccentric Star, Box Quilt.

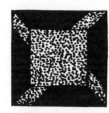 2086. Captain's Wheel

 2087. Captain's Wheel

 2088. Slashed Album

 2089. Valley Forge Quilt

 2090. Unknown

 2091. Unknown

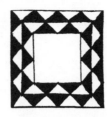 2092. Our Village Green

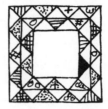 2093. Ocean Waves

 2094. Ocean

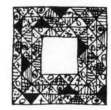 2095. Unknown

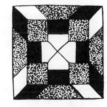 2096. Unknown

 2097. Unknown

 2098. Springtime

 2104. Unknown

 2099. Unknown

 2105. Unknown

 2100. Pinwheel Skew

 2106. Unknown

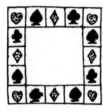 2101. Bridge Patch

 2107. Unknown

 2102. Springfield

 2108. Bay Leaf (pieced and appliquéd)

 2103. Unknown

 2109. Tangled Lines

 2110. White House Steps

 2111. Arkansas

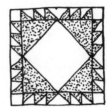 2112. Unknown

 2113. Thunder Clouds

 2114. Fox and Geese

 2115. Nine-patch

 2116. Goose Tracks Variation

2117. Framed Medallion

 2118. Sunshine

 2119. Blindman's Fancy

 2120. Sawtooth

2121. Jagged Edge

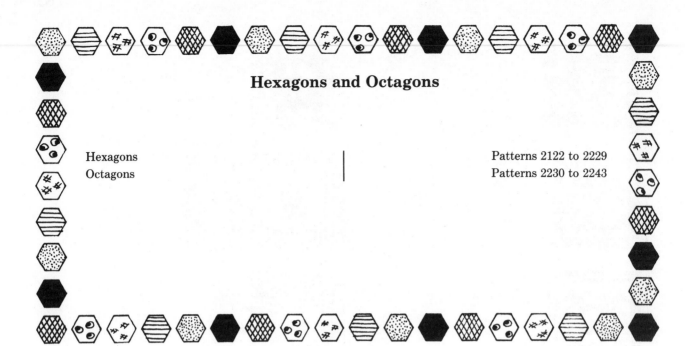

Hexagons and Octagons

Hexagons
Octagons

Patterns 2122 to 2229
Patterns 2230 to 2243

2122. Variegated Hexagon*

2123. Century†

2124. Flower Garden

2125. The Old-fashioned Wheel Quilt

2126. Unknown

2127. A Hexagon

* *Also:* Poor Boy (small).
† *Also:* Hexagon Patch, Giant Maxigon.

2128. Snowflake*

2129. Unknown

2130. Spinning Patches

2131. Unknown

2132. Unknown

2133. Wonder of Egypt

2134. Wonder of Egypt

2135. Orange Peel

2136. Unknown

2137. Unknown

2138. Snow Crystal

2139. Hexagon Garden

* *Also:* Basket, Bride's Bouquet.

2140. Mosaic

2141. Mosaic

2142. Grandmother's Flower Garden

2143. Grandmother's Flower Garden

2144. Grandmother's Flower Garden

2145. Grandmother's Flower Garden*

2146. Grandma Bell's Flower Garden

2147. Grandmother's Flower Garden

2148. Flower Garden with Diamond

2149. Grandmother's Flower Garden

2150. Flower Garden†

2151. Flower Garden (with green leaves)

* *Also:* Honeycomb.
† *Also:* Grandma's Flower Garden, Grandma's Garden, French Nosegay, Mosaic, Dime-size Flower Garden (when small).

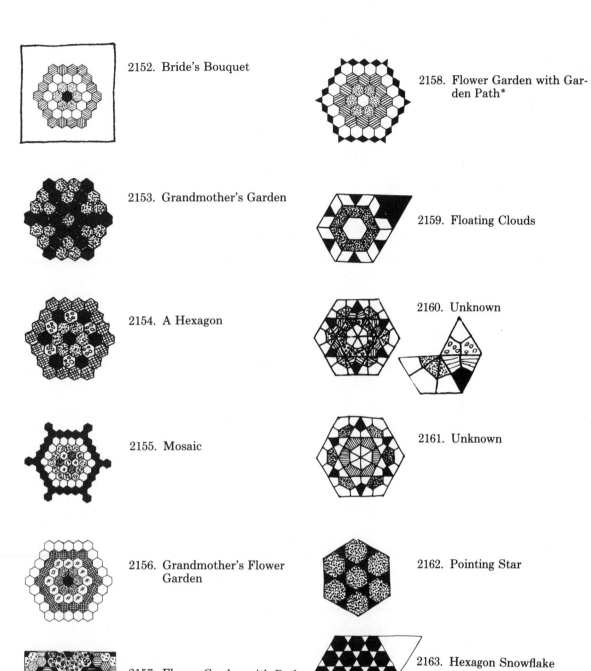

2152. Bride's Bouquet

2153. Grandmother's Garden

2154. A Hexagon

2155. Mosaic

2156. Grandmother's Flower Garden

2157. Flower Garden with Paths

2158. Flower Garden with Garden Path*

2159. Floating Clouds

2160. Unknown

2161. Unknown

2162. Pointing Star

2163. Hexagon Snowflake

* *Also:* Martha Washington's Flower Garden.

2164. Flower

2165. Solomon's Garden

2166. Unknown

2167. Unknown

2168. Unknown

2169. Basket of Flowers

2170. Basket of Flowers

2171. Basket of Flowers

2172. The Flower Basket

2173. Honeycomb

2174. Mosaic

2175. Fields of Diamonds

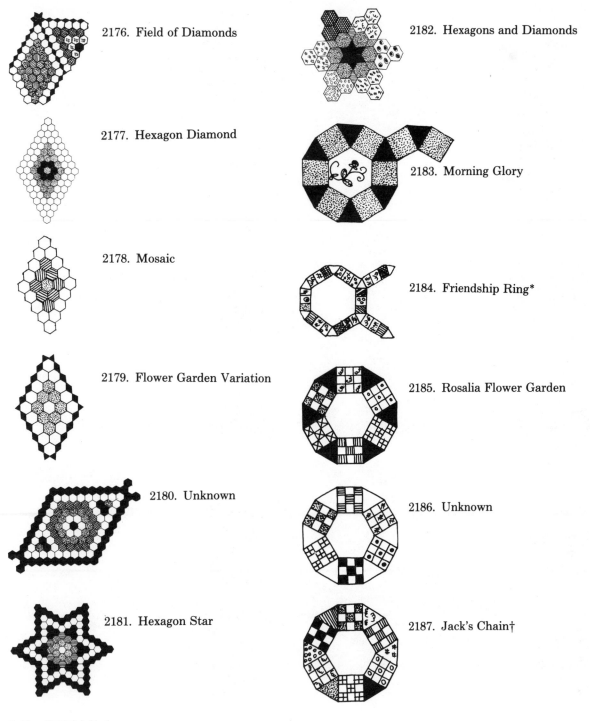

2176. Field of Diamonds

2177. Hexagon Diamond

2178. Mosaic

2179. Flower Garden Variation

2180. Unknown

2181. Hexagon Star

2182. Hexagons and Diamonds

2183. Morning Glory

2184. Friendship Ring*

2185. Rosalia Flower Garden

2186. Unknown

2187. Jack's Chain†

* *Also:* Faithful Circle.
† *Also:* Rosalia Flower Garden.

2188. Florida

2194. Madison Quilt

2189. New Hampshire

2195. Hexagon Star

2190. Florida

2196. Hexagon Star

2191. Kentucky

2197. Unknown

2192. Madison

2198. Unknown

2193. The Madison Block

2199. Dutch Tile

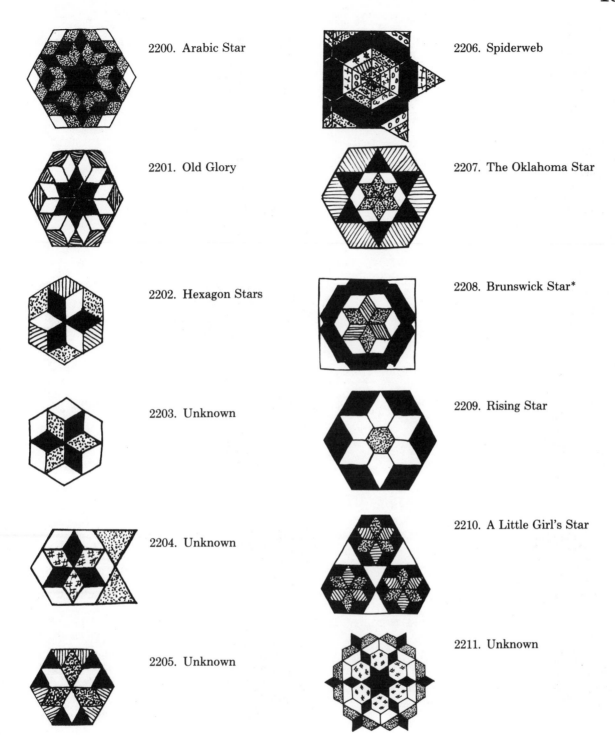

2200. Arabic Star

2201. Old Glory

2202. Hexagon Stars

2203. Unknown

2204. Unknown

2205. Unknown

2206. Spiderweb

2207. The Oklahoma Star

2208. Brunswick Star*

2209. Rising Star

2210. A Little Girl's Star

2211. Unknown

* *Also:* Rolling Star, Chained Star.

2212. The Pyramid

2218. Unknown

2213. Ocean Wave

2219. Unknown

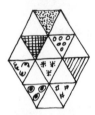

2214. The Mowing Machine Quilt

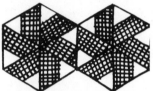

2220. Whirligig Hexagon

2215. Block Patchwork

2221. Star and Crescent*

2216. The Mending Wall

2222. Unknown

2217. Unknown

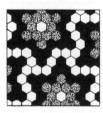

2223. Star Hexagon

* *Also:* Twinkling Star.

2224. Flower Garden Operation

2225. Merry-Go-Round

2226. Ocean Wave

2227. Diamond Mine

2228. Diamond Mine

2229. Mosaic*

2230. Golden Gates

2231. Stop Sign

2232. Unknown

2233. Montana

2234. Unknown

2235. Wheel of Fortune

* *Also:* Rainbow Tile, Diamond Field.

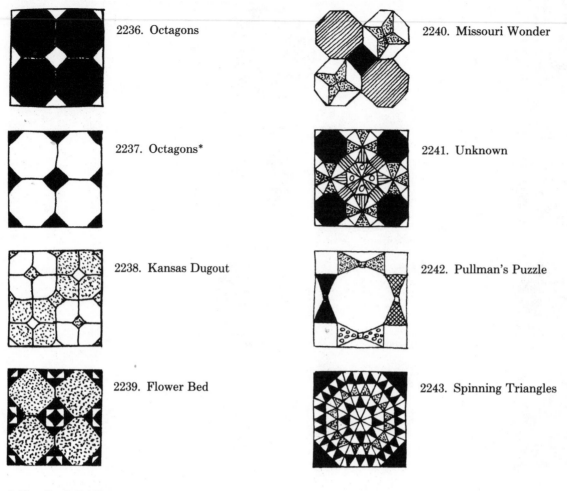

2236. Octagons

2240. Missouri Wonder

2237. Octagons*

2241. Unknown

2238. Kansas Dugout

2242. Pullman's Puzzle

2239. Flower Bed

2243. Spinning Triangles

* *Also:* Ozark Cobblestones.

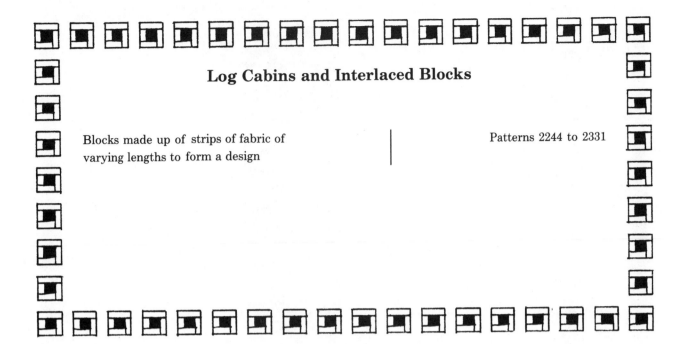

Log Cabins and Interlaced Blocks

Blocks made up of strips of fabric of varying lengths to form a design

Patterns 2244 to 2331

2244. American Log Patchwork (basic block)

2245. Simple Log Cabin Arrangement

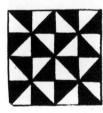

2246. Pinwheel Arrangement

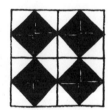

2247. Sunshine and Shadow Arrangement

2248. Zigzag Arrangement

2249. Square with Ring Arrangement

2250. Barn-raising Arrangement

2256. Unknown Arrangement

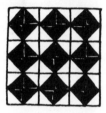

2251. Straight Furrows Arrangement

2257. Unknown Arrangement

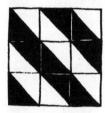

2252. Courthouse Steps Arrangement

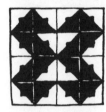

2258. Unknown Arrangement

2253. Light and Dark Arrangement*

2259. Unknown Arrangement

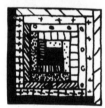

2254. Log Cabin

2260. Log Cabin

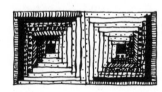

2255. Barn Raising

2261. Log Cabin

* *Also:* Sunlight and Shadow Arrangement, Sunlight and Shadow.

 2262. Fine-woven Patch

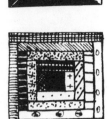 2268. Basic Block

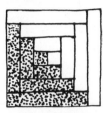 2263. Log Cabin

 2269. Unknown

 2264. Unknown

 2270. Log Cabin

 2265. Log Cabin

 2271. Log Cabin

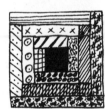 2266. Log Cabin

 2272. Log Cabin

 2267. Log Cabin

2273. Log Cabin*

* *Also:* Cabin in the Cotton.

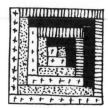 2274. Unknown

 2280. Log Cabin

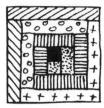 2275. Log Cabin

 2281. Courthouse Steps

 2276. Log Cabin

 2282. Log Cabin

 2277. Log Cabin

 2283. Log Cabin

 2278. White House Steps

 2284. Unknown

 2279. Crayon Box (each piece plain bright color)

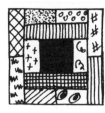 2285. English Log Cabin (four blocks shown)

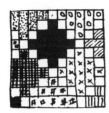 2286. Jake Mast

 2292. Pineapples Arrangements*

 2287. Courthouse Steps

 2293. Pineapples†

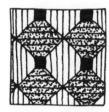 2288. Coarse-woven Patchwork

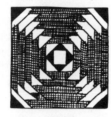 2294. Maltese Cross

 2289. Log Cabin

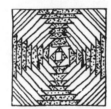 2295. Windmill Blades

 2290. White House Steps

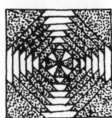 2296. Pineapple‡

 2291. The Log Patch

 2297. Pineapple

* *Also:* Chestnut Burr.
†*Also:* Wild Goose Chase.
‡ *Also:* Maltese Cross.

198

 2298. Pineapple Block

 2299. Pineapple

 2300. Pineapple (number of rounds vary)

 2301. Church Steps

 2302. Burr Wheel

 2303. Church Steps

 2304. Maltese Cross

 2305. Turning Wheels

 2306. Maltese Cross

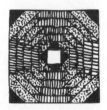 2307. Maltese Cross

 2308. The Pineapple

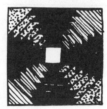 2309. Amish Pineapple

 2310. Maltese Cross

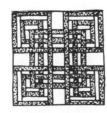 2316. The Gordian Knot

 2311. Interlaced Blocks

 2317. Gordian Knot

 2312. Interlaced Blocks

 2318. All Tangled Up*

 2313. Carpenter's Square

 2319. Kentucky Chain

 2314. Carpenter's Square

 2320. Interlocked Squares

 2315. Carpenter's Square

 2321. Strip Squares

* *Also:* Mystic Maze.

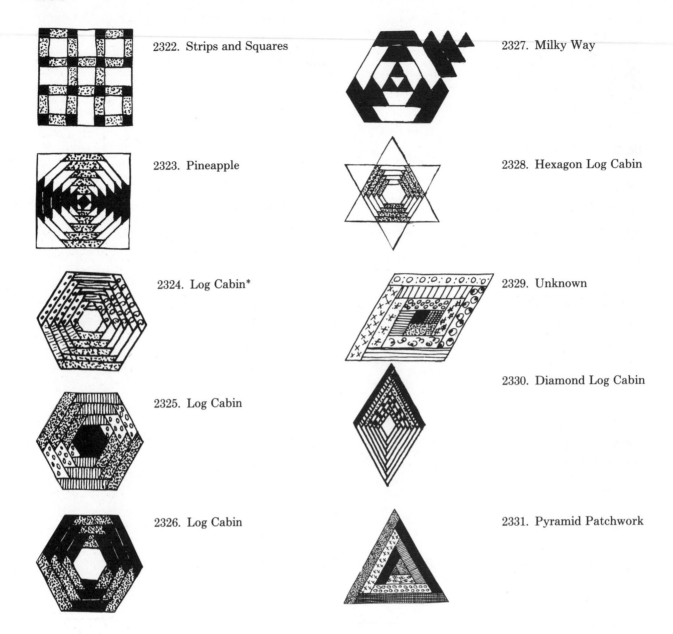

2322. Strips and Squares

2323. Pineapple

2324. Log Cabin*

2325. Log Cabin

2326. Log Cabin

2327. Milky Way

2328. Hexagon Log Cabin

2329. Unknown

2330. Diamond Log Cabin

2331. Pyramid Patchwork

* *Also:* Star Cabin.

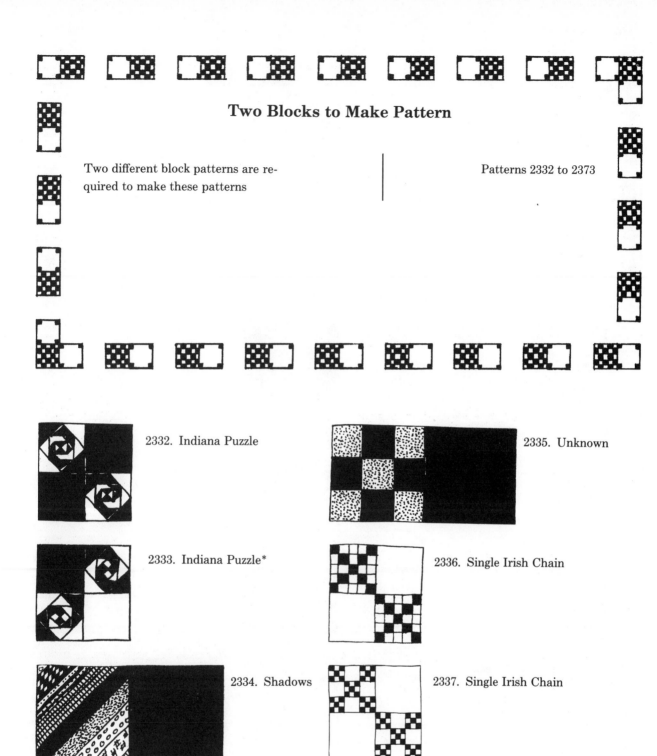

Two Blocks to Make Pattern

Two different block patterns are required to make these patterns

Patterns 2332 to 2373

2332. Indiana Puzzle

2333. Indiana Puzzle*

2334. Shadows

2335. Unknown

2336. Single Irish Chain

2337. Single Irish Chain

* *Also:* Virginia Reel, Monkey Wrench, Snail's Trail.

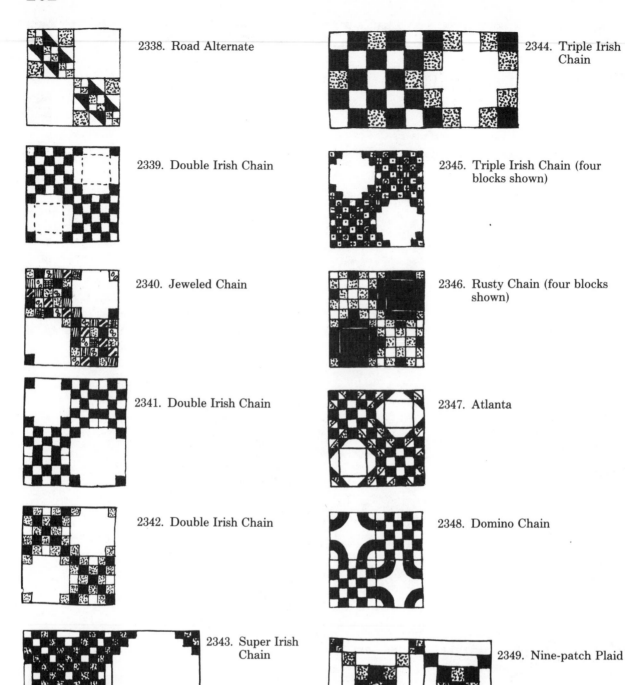

2338. Road Alternate

2339. Double Irish Chain

2340. Jeweled Chain

2341. Double Irish Chain

2342. Double Irish Chain

2343. Super Irish Chain

2344. Triple Irish Chain

2345. Triple Irish Chain (four blocks shown)

2346. Rusty Chain (four blocks shown)

2347. Atlanta

2348. Domino Chain

2349. Nine-patch Plaid

 2350. The Modern Broken Dish

 2356. Railroad Crossing

 2351. Country Gardens

 2357. Jack-in-the-Box

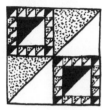 2352. Unknown (four blocks shown)

 2358. Wedding Ring Tile

 2353. Kaleidoscope (four blocks shown)

 2359. Pointed tile

 2354. Rock Garden (four blocks shown)

 2360. Shoofly Block (four blocks shown)

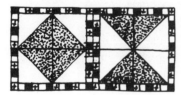 2355. Crossroads

 2361. Churn Dash

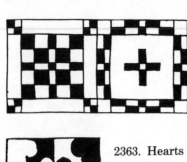

2362. The Square
and Cross

2368. Four-patch
Quilt

2363. Hearts and Gizzards

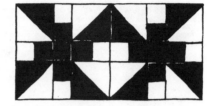

2369. Broken
Arrow

2364. Unknown (four blocks
shown)

2370. Mexican
Star

2365. World without End (four
blocks shown)

2371. The Old Woman's Road

2366. Interlocking
Windmills

2372. Square within a Square

2367. World
without End

2373. Winding Ways*

* *Also:* Nashville, Tennessee Circle, Robbing Peter to Pay Paul, Wheel of Mystery.

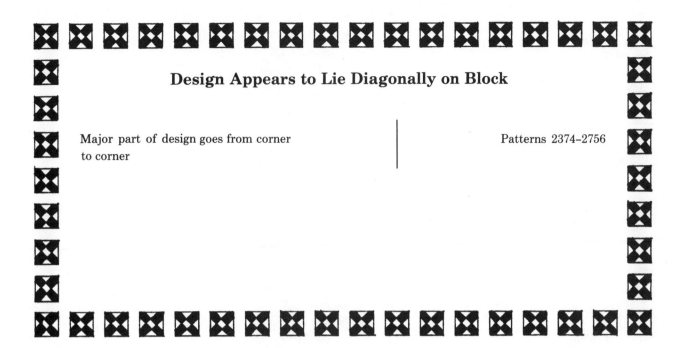

Design Appears to Lie Diagonally on Block

Major part of design goes from corner to corner

Patterns 2374–2756

2374. Double Triangle

2377. Railroad Crossing (four blocks shown)

2375. Lady of the Lake

2378. Railroad Crossing

2376. Birds in the Air

2379. Lady of the Lake

 2380. Wild Goose Chase

 2386. Wild Goose Chase

2381. Railroad Crossing

 2387. Wild Goose Flight

2382. Railroad Crossing

 2388. Unknown

2383. Wild Goose Chase

 2389. Wild Goose Chase

 2384. Toad in a Puddle*

 2390. Unknown

 2385. Odd Fellows†

 2391. Wild Goose Chase‡

* *Also:* Jack-in-the-Pulpit.
† *Also:* Wild Goose Chase.
‡ *Also:* Flying Geese.

 2392. Wild Goose Chase

 2398. Wild Goose Chase

 2393. Unknown

 2399. Odd Fellow's Patch

 2394. Odd Fellow's Patch

 2400. Wild Goose Block

 2395. The Wild Goose Chase*

 2401. Wild Goose Block

 2396. Wild Goose Chase

 2402. Old Maid's Ramble

 2397. Wild Goose Chase

 2403. The Rambler†

* *Also:* Odd Fellow's Patch.
† *Also:* Crimson Rambler.

2404. Rambler*

2405. Rambler

2406. I X L†

2407. Flying Geese

2408. Wild Geese‡

2409. The Ozark Trail

2410. Flying Geese

2411. A Snowflake

2412. A Snowflake

2413. Unknown

2414. Unknown

2415. Unknown

* *Also:* Spring Beauty.
† *Also:* I Excel.
‡ *Also:* Double T.

2416. Mosaic

2417. Unknown

2418. The Mountain Peak

2419. Autograph Patch

2420. The House Jack Built

2421. At the Depot*

2422. Chuck-a-Luck

2423. Autograph Quilt

2424. At the Depot†

2425. Cross

2426. Railroad Crossing

2427. Unknown

* *Also:* Autograph Quilt, Railroad Crossing, Railroad Tracks, The House Jack Built.
† *Also:* Autograph Quilt, Railroad Crossing, Railroad Tracks.

2428. Next-door Neighbor

2429. Mosaic

2430. Malvinea's Chain

2431. Unknown

2432. Odd Tippecanoe

2433. Old Tippecanoe*

2434. Old Tippecanoe

2435. Royal Star†

2436. Royal Star

2437. Royal Star

2438. Centennial

2439. Centennial

* *Also:* Tippecanoe and Tyler, too.
† *Also:* Star.

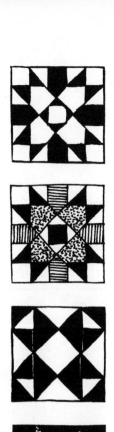

2440. Providence Quilt

2441. Providence Quilt Block

2442. Mosaic

2443. Missouri Star

2444. Air Castle

2445. Cat and Mice

2446. Cats and Mice

2447. Cats and Mice

2448. Heather Square

2449. King's Crown

2450. Swing in the Center

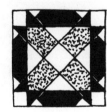

2451. The Three Crosses

2452. Joseph's Coat*

2458. Union Square†

2453. Domino and Square

2459. Union Square

2454. Domino and Square

2460. Bear Paw

2455. Domino and Squares

2461. Union Square

2456. Joseph's Coat

2462. Mary's Squares

2457. Joseph's Coat

2463. Vermont

*Also: Scrap Bag.
†Also: Mosaic.

 2464. Boxes

 2465. Cross

 2466. Children of Israel

 2467. Children of Israel

 2468. Gentleman's Fancy

2469. Handy Andy

 2470. Joseph's Coat

 2471. Swing in the Corner

 2472. Greek Cross

 2473. Saddlebag

 2474. Double T

 2475. Sawtooth

2476. Another Sawtooth

2482. Augusta

2477. Secret Drawer*

2483. Unknown

2478. Mosaic

2484. The Royal

2479. Unknown

2485. Royal Cross

2480. Arkansas Traveler

2486. Raleigh

2481. Unknown

2487. Royal Cross

* *Also:* Spools, Arkansas Traveler.

2488. Hunter's Horn

2489. Sun, Moon, and Stars

2490. Dutch Mill

2491. Dutch Mill

2492. Christian Cross

2493. Album Quilt

2494. Washington Sidewalk

2495. Unknwon

2496. Washington Sidewalk

2497. Album

2498. Red Cross

2499. Unknown

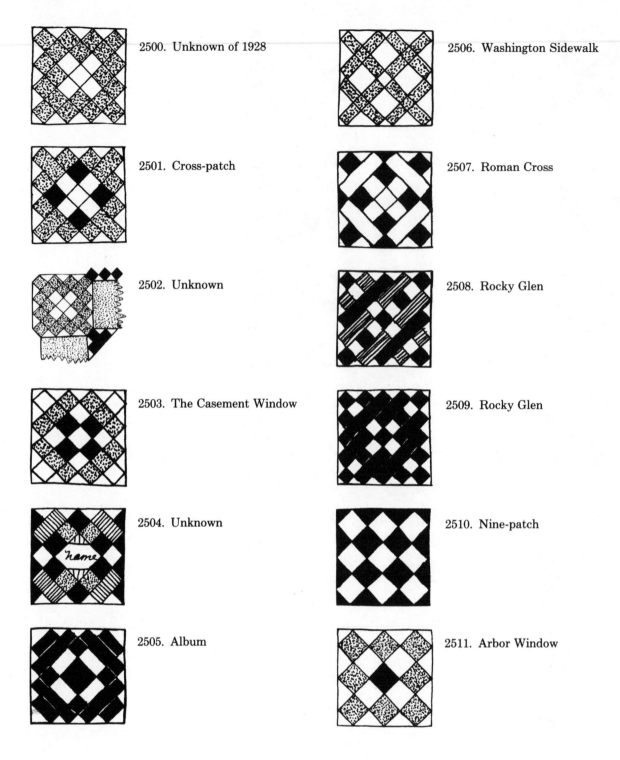

2500. Unknown of 1928

2501. Cross-patch

2502. Unknown

2503. The Casement Window

2504. Unknown

2505. Album

2506. Washington Sidewalk

2507. Roman Cross

2508. Rocky Glen

2509. Rocky Glen

2510. Nine-patch

2511. Arbor Window

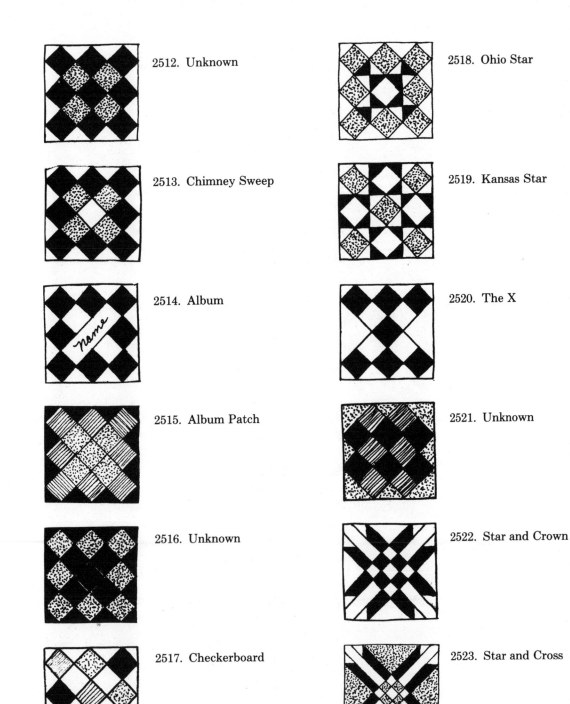

2512. Unknown

2513. Chimney Sweep

2514. Album

2515. Album Patch

2516. Unknown

2517. Checkerboard

2518. Ohio Star

2519. Kansas Star

2520. The X

2521. Unknown

2522. Star and Crown

2523. Star and Cross

2524. Mexican Cross

2525. The Mexican Star

2526. Mexican Rose*

2527. Crossroads to Texas†

2528. Nine-patch Star

2529. Chain of Diamonds

2530. Flowering Nine-patch

2531. Flowering Nine-patch

2532. Square and Swallow

2533. Swinging Corners

2534. Wandering Foot‡

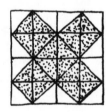

2535. Old Tippecanoe

* *Also:* Mexican Star.
† *Also:* Crossed Roads to Texas.
‡ *Also:* Turkey Track.

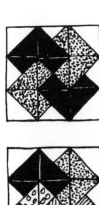 2536. Card Trick

 2542. Castle in Air

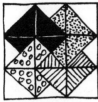 2537. Card Trick

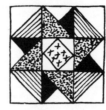 2543. Air Castle

 2538. Card Trick

 2544. Card Tricks

2539. Four Playing Stones

 2545. Grandma's Hopscotch

 2540. Card Tricks

 2546. Square and Swallow*

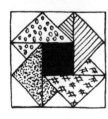 2541. Color Wheel

 2547. Bleeding Heart

* *Also:* Bleeding Heart.

 2548. Bleeding Heart

 2554. Farmer's Daughter

 2549. Bleeding Heart

 2555. Domino

 2550. Mrs. Ewer's Tulip (pieced and appliquéd)

 2556. Star in a Star

 2551. Jack's Blocks

 2557. Dove in the Window

 2552. Corner Posts

 2558. Dove in the Window

 2553. Corner Posts

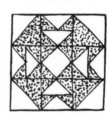 2559. T Block

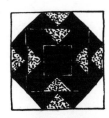 2560. Imperial T*

 2566. Four T's

 2561. Capital T

 2567. Helen's Choice

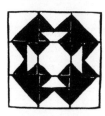 2562. Imperial T

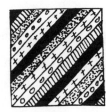 2568. String Quilt

 2563. T

 2569. The Friendship Name Quilt

 2564. Boxed

 2570. Attic Window

 2565. Texas Tears

 2571. Unknown

*Also: Double T.

 2572. Unknown

 2578. Queen Charlotte's Crown†

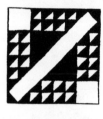 2573. Primrose Path

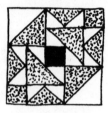 2579. Unknown

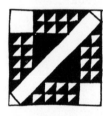 2574. Primrose Path

 2580. Queen Charlotte's Crown

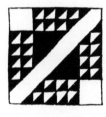 2575. Bismarck

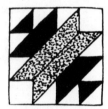 2581. Mrs. Taft's Choice

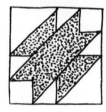 2576. The Anvil*

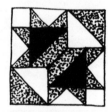 2582. Queen Charlotte's Crown

 2577. Queen Charlotte's Crown

 2583. Queen Charlotte's Crown‡

* *Also:* Anvil.
† *Also:* Indian Meadow.
‡ *Also:* Indian Meadow.

 2584. Queen Charlotte's Crown*

 2590. Interlocking Windmill

 2585. St. Andrew's Cross

 2591. Kaleidoscope

 2586. Unknown

 2592. Mayflower

 2587. Autograph Cross

 2593. Mayflower

 2588. The Cotton Ball Quilt

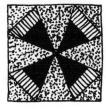 2594. Kaleidoscope Variation

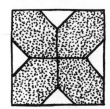 2589. Unknown

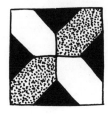 2595. Kaleidoscope Variation

* *Also:* Indian Meadow.

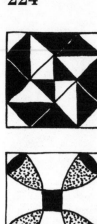 2596. Next-door Neighbor

 2602. Propeller

 2597. The President Roosevelt

 2603. Endless Chain

 2598. The Windmill

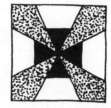 2604. The Pinwheel

2599. Unknown

 2605. Nevada

 2600. Dutch Mill

 2606. Sunshiny Day

 2601. Nine-patch Kaleidoscope

 2607. Unknown

2608. Indian Hatchet

2609. Devil's Puzzle

2610. Crossroads

2611. Alphabet L

2612. Primrose Path

2613. Michigan

2614. Mary Tenny Grey Travel Club Patch

2615. Brick Pavements

2616. Brick Pavement

2617. Cross and Crown

2618. Cross and Crown

2619. The Three Crosses

 2620. Cats and Mice

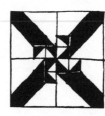 2626. Mrs. Morgan's Choice

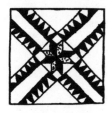 2621. New York Beauty

 2627. Railroad Crossing

 2622. Honolulu

 2628. Pinwheel

 2623. Grape Vines

 2629. Unknown

 2624. Unknown

 2630. Memory Blocks

 2625. Wood Lily

 2631. Unknown

 2632. Unknown

 2633. This and That

 2634. The Pyramids

 2635. Grandmother's Cross

 2636. Grandmother's Cross

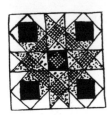 2637. Joseph's Coat

 2638. Joseph's Coat

 2639. Gentleman's Fancy

 2640. Nonsense

 2641. Lincoln

 2642. Mountain Homestead

 2643. Modified Wheel of Fortune

2644. Wheel of Fortune*

2645. Wheel of Fortune

2646. Scrap Bag Squares

2647. Phoenix

2648. Boxes

2649. Delectable Mountains

 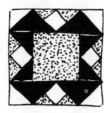  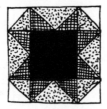 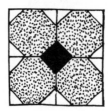 

2650. Handy Andy

2651. Salt Lake City

2652. Mosaic

2653. Sawtooth Star

2654. The Four-leaf Clover

2655. Mosaic Variation

* *Also:* Buttons and Bows, Rising Sun.

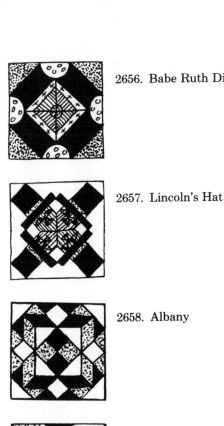 2656. Babe Ruth Diamond

2657. Lincoln's Hat

2658. Albany

2659. Dover

2660. Dover Quilt Block

2661. Arkansas

 2662. Maine

 2663. Arkansas

 2664. Jackknife Block

 2665. Devil's Claws*

 2666. Devil's Claws†

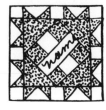 2667. Cluster of Lilies

* *Also:* Des Moines, Botch-handle, The Crow Foot.
† *Also:* Lily.

 2668. Autumn Leaf

 2674. Small Diagonal Checker-board

 2669. Four Crowns

 2675. Nine-patch*

 2670. Union Star

 2676. Checkerboard Squares

 2671. Unknown

 2677. Checkerboard and Pinwheels (four blocks shown)

 2672. Unknown

 2678. Dublin Chain

 2673. Unknown

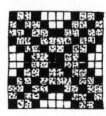 2679. Steps to the Garden

* *Also:* Checkerboard.

 2680. Road to California (four blocks shown)

 2686. Evening Star with an Evening Star*

 2681. Providence

 2687. Sara's Star

 2682. Fool's Square

 2688. Free Trade Block

 2683. Unknown

 2689. St. Paul

 2684. Providence

 2690. Annapolis

 2685. King David's Crown

 2691. Century of Progress

* *Also:* Odd Fellow's Chain, San Diego.

 2692. Lover's Knot

 2698. All Kinds

 2693. Annapolis Star

 2699. The Rainbow Square

 2694. All Kinds

 2700. Lover's Knot

 2695. Domino

 2701. Ancient Castle

 2696. Turnabout T

 2702. Crossed Arrows

 2697. Farmer's Field

 2703. Railroad Crossing

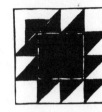

2704. Railroad Crossing

2705. Devil's Claw

2706. Devil's Claws

2707. Lily Quilt

2708. The Corner Star

2709. The Anvil

2710. Anvil

2711. The Swallow

2712. Lighthouse

2713. Square and a Half

2714. Little Rock

2715. Olympia

2716. Unknown

2717. Unknown

2718. Key West Star

2719. Buckwheat

2720. Christian Cross

2721. New Frontier

2722. Memory Block

2723. St. Greg. Cross

2724. Propeller

2725. Alaska

2726. Morning Glory

2727. Jefferson City

 2728. The Old Windmill

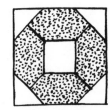 2734. The Wishing Ring

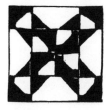 2729. Columbia Puzzle

 2735. David and Goliath

 2730. Venetian Design

 2736. Full-blown Tulip

 2731. Nine-patch Star

 2737. Old Missouri

 2732. The Spiderweb

 2738. Trenton Block

 2733. Corn and Beans Variation

 2739. Spiderweb

 2740. Home Treasure

 2746. Wagon Wheels

 2741. Persian

 2747. Wedding Ring Bouquet

 2742. Star Flower

 2748. Arab Tent

 2743. Missouri Star

 2749. Blue Bars, Gray Bars, No Stars

 2744. The Secret Drawer

 2750. Charleston

 2745. South Carolina

 2751. Friendship Links

 2752. Virginia Reel

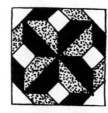 2755. Shaded Trail

 2753. Hazel Valley Crossroads

 2756. New Jersey

 2754. Fish in a Dish (four blocks shown)

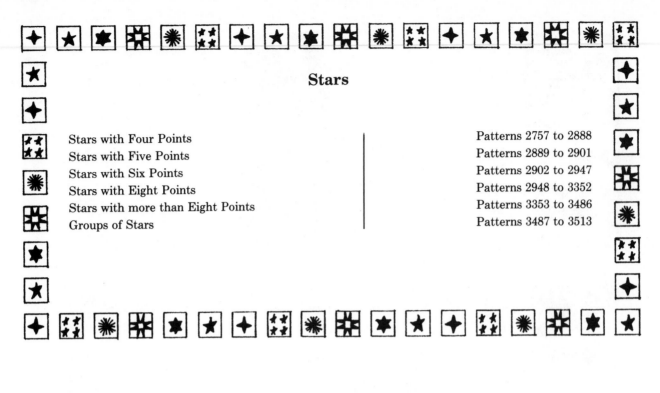

Stars

Stars with Four Points	Patterns 2757 to 2888
Stars with Five Points	Patterns 2889 to 2901
Stars with Six Points	Patterns 2902 to 2947
Stars with Eight Points	Patterns 2948 to 3352
Stars with more than Eight Points	Patterns 3353 to 3486
Groups of Stars	Patterns 3487 to 3513

2757. Arkansas Snow Flake

2760. Snowball

2758. Four Points*

2761. The Kite Quilt

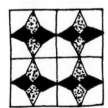

2759. Job's Tears

2762. The Four-pointed Star

* *Also:* Periwinkle, Hummingbird, Arkansas Star, Four-point Kite, Job's Trouble, Arkansas Snowflake, Snowball, Snowflake, Four-pointed Star, Pontiac Star, Star Kites.

 2763. Four-pointed Star

 2769. Unknown

 2764. Tel Star

 2770. The Pine Burr

 2765. Rebecca's Star

 2771. The Philippines

 2766. Rock Garden

 2772. Philadelphia Patch

 2767. Cockleburr

 2773. Pineapple Cactus

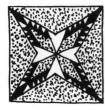 2768. Feathered World without End

 2774. Phillippines

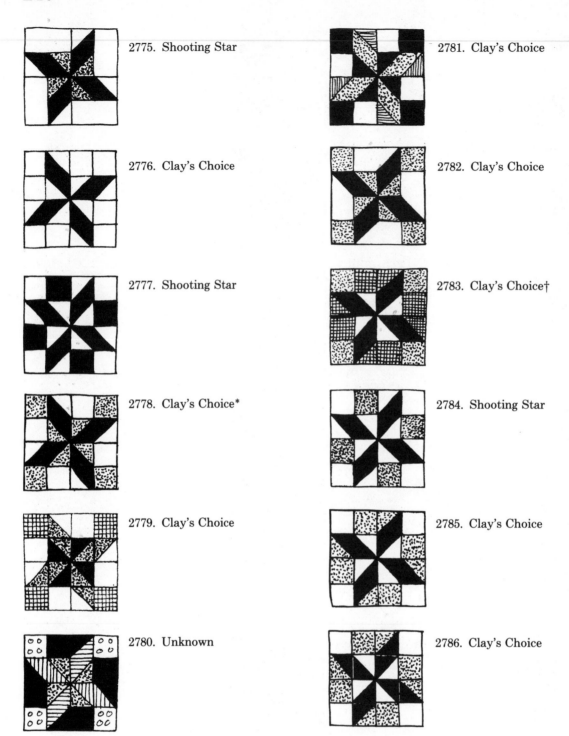

2775. Shooting Star

2781. Clay's Choice

2776. Clay's Choice

2782. Clay's Choice

2777. Shooting Star

2783. Clay's Choice†

2778. Clay's Choice*

2784. Shooting Star

2779. Clay's Choice

2785. Clay's Choice

2780. Unknown

2786. Clay's Choice

* *Also:* Harry's Star, Henry of the West, Star of the West, Jackson's Star.
† *Also:* Shooting Star.

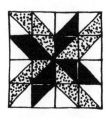 2787. Constellation

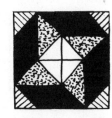 2793. Next-door Neighbor

 2788. Star Puzzle

 2794. July Fourth

 2789. The North Star

 2795. Unknown

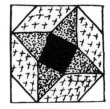 2790. Unknown

 2796. Dove in the Window

 2791. Friendship Star

 2797. Unknown

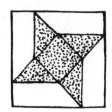 2792. Unknown

 2798. Cowboy's Star

 2799. Arkansas Traveler

 2805. King's Crown†

 2800. Arkansas Traveler

 2806. Alaska Chinook‡

 2801. Harlequin Star

 2807. The Four Winds

 2802. Rockingham's Beauty

 2808. Four Winds§

 2803. Star and Crescent

 2809. Star and Crescent

 2804. Star of the West*

 2810. Kaleidoscope

* *Also:* Compass, Four Winds.
† *Also:* The Four Winds.
‡ *Also:* The Four Winds, Star of the Four Winds, Star and Crescent, Lucky Star.
§ *Also:* Alaska Chinook, The Four Winds, Star of the Four Winds, Star and Crescent.

 2811. Kaleidoscopic Patch

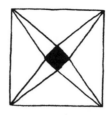 2817. Kaleidoscope

 2812. World without End

 2818. Priscilla

 2813. Great Circle

 2819. World without End

 2814. Geometric Star

 2820. Windmill Star

 2815. Skyrocket*

 2821. Unknown

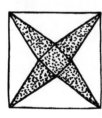 2816. Rocky Road to Kansas

 2822. Diane's Four-pointed Star

* *Also:* Skyrocket Pad.

 2823. Exploding Stars

 2824. Lost Children

 2825. Texas Ranger

 2826. Unknown

 2827. Iowa Star

 2828. Rocky Road to Kansas

 2829. Rocky Road to Kansas

 2830. Rocky Road to Kansas

 2831. Rocky Road to Kansas

 2832. String Star Quilt

 2833. Beautiful Star

 2834. Beautiful Star

 2835. Tippecanoe

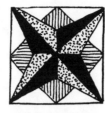 2841. Star

 2836. Crossed Canoes

 2842. Unknown

 2837. The Dragonfly

 2843. Odd Star

 2838. Unknown

 2844. Hattie's Choice

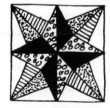 2839. Mother's Delight

 2845. Key West Star

 2840. Eight-pointed Star

 2846. Key West Beauty

 2847. Key West Beauty

 2853. Heart's Desire

 2848. Morning Star

 2854. Heart's Desire

 2849. Morning Star

 2855. Skyrocket

 2850. Morning Star

 2856. Blazing Star

 2851. Kaleidoscope

 2857. The Kite

 2852. Morning Star

 2858. Golda, Gem Star

 2859. Four Winds

 2865. Four-leaf Clover

 2860. Star and Crown

 2866. Boston

 2861. Wisconsin

 2867. Concord

 2862. Unknown

 2868. Boston

 2863. Unknown

 2869. Wildflower

 2864. Unknown

 2870. Cypress

2871. Unknown

2877. The Star Sapphire

2872. Guiding Star

2878. Time and Tide (four blocks shown)

2873. King David's Crown

2879. Star of Mystery

2874. Barbara Bannister's Star

2880. Edna's Triumph

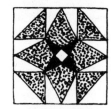

2875. Butterfly Block

2881. A Star

2876. Star

2882. Shaded Trail

 2883. Ella's Star

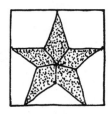 2889. Five-pointed Star

 2884. Unknown

 2890. Starflower

 2885. The Fenced-in Star

 2891. Unknown

 2886. Vice President

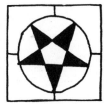 2892. Star of the West

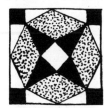 2887. Her Sparkling Jewels

 2893. Texas

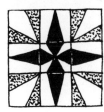 2888. The Guiding Star

 2894. Union Star

250

 2895. Union Star

 2901. The Broken Crown

 2896. Bicentennial Star

 2902. The Seven Sisters Quilt

 2897. Bicentennial Star

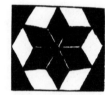 2903. Hexagonal Star*

 2898. Evening Star

 2904. Builder's Blocks

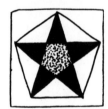 2899. Unknown

 2905. Unknown

 2900. Mountain Pink

 2906. Diamond Star

* *Also:* Hexagonal.

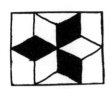 2907. Novel Star

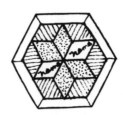 2913. Friendship Quilt

 2908. Star of the East

 2914. Columbia

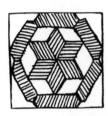 2909. Brunswick Star

 2915. Field Flowers

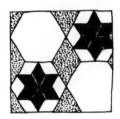 2910. Rise and Shine

 2916. Star and Planets

 2911. Pathway to the Star

 2917. Savannah Beautiful Star

 2912. Unknown

 2918. Florida Star

2919. Glory Block

2925. Unknown

2920. Six-pointed Star

2926. Texas Star

2921. Rainbow Star

2927. Dolly Madison Pattern

2922. Six-point Star

2928. Texas Star

2923. Star of Bethlehem

2929. Texas Star

2924. Bobbins*

2930. Hex Star

* *Also*: Star of Bethlehem.

 2931. Unknown

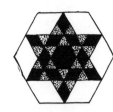 2937. Ozark Diamonds*

 2932. Evening Star

 2938. Unknown

 2933. Arrowheads

 2939. Star of Bethlehem

 2934. Unknown

 2940. Six-pointed Star

 2935. Aunt Martha's Rose

 2941. Savannah†

 2936. Ma Perkins' Flower Garden

 2942. Chained Star

* *Also:* Ozark Diamond, Ozark Star.
† *Also:* Beautiful Star.

 2943. Diamond Beauty

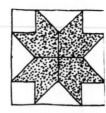 2949. Star of LeMoyne

 2944. Colorado

 2950. Unknown

 2945. Unknown

 2951. Unknown

 2946. Cosmos

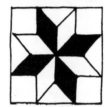 2952. LeMoyne Star†

 2947. Tumbling Blocks

 2953. Diamond‡

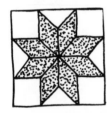 2948. Eight-pointed Star*

 2954. Unknown

* *Also:* LeMoyne Star, Lemon Star, Star of LeMoyne.
† *Also:* Eight-diamond Star Quilt, Lemon Star, Star of LeMoyne.
‡ *Also:* Eight-pointed Star.

 2955. King's Crown

 2956. Star Block

 2957. LeMoyne Star

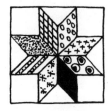 2958. Rebecca's Five Star Nine-patch

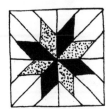 2959. Shasta Daisy

 2960. Star of the Milky Way*

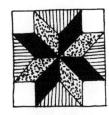 2961. Unknown

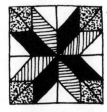 2962. Columns

 2963. Eight-point Star

 2964. Sunlight and Shadows

 2965. Columbus

 2966. Evening Star

* *Also:* Square and Compass.

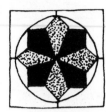 2967. Purple Cross

 2973. Silver and Gold

 2968. Purple Cross

 2974. Twinkling Star

 2969. The Purple Cross

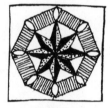 2975. Unknown

 2970. LeMoyne Star

 2976. The Whirling Star

 2971. Star of LeMoyne

 2977. Sunbeam

 2972. Silver and Gold

 2978. The Sunbeam Block

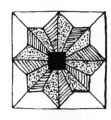 2979. Sunbeam

 2985. Blazing Star

 2980. Sunbeam Block

 2986. Blazing Star

 2981. Missouri Daisy

 2987. St. Louis*

 2982. Friendship Star

 2988. Blazing Star

 2983. Album Blocks

 2989. Blazing Star

 2984. Friendship Star

 2990. Star†

* *Also:* Compass.
† *Also:* Blazing Star.

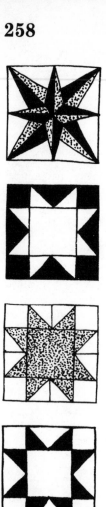

2991. Blazing Star

 2997. Magic Cross

2992. Eight-pointed Star Quilt*

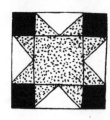 2998. Austin

2993. Eight-pointed Star

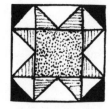 2999. Sawtooth Star

2994. Evening Star†

 3000. Unknown

2995. Evening Star

 3001. A New Star is Born

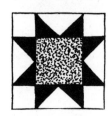 2996. Sawtooth

 3002. Pinwheel

* *Also:* Sawtoothed Star.
† *Also:* Simple Star.

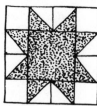

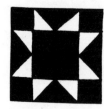

 3003. Octagonal Star

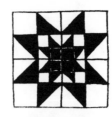 3009. The Rising Star

 3004. Martha Washington*

 3010. Eight Hands Round

 3005. Rising Star

 3011. Rising Star

 3006. Eight Hands Round

 3012. Rising Star‡

 3007. Stars and Squares

 3013. Star in a Star

 3008. Rising Star†

 3014. Indian Star

* *Also:* Pierced Star.
† *Also:* Star and Squares.
‡ *Also:* Star and Square.

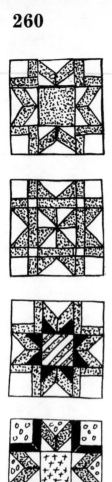

3015. Morning Star

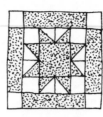

3021. Eight-pointed Star

3016. Star Lane

3022. Eight-pointed Star with Frame

3017. Virginia

3023. Mother's Fancy

3018. Morning Star

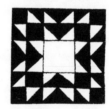

3024. Unknown

3019. Columbian Star

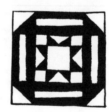

3025. Unknown

3020. Chicago Star

3026. Burnham Square

 3027. Hole in the Barn Door with Eight-pointed Star

 3033. Aunt Eliza Star

 3028. Eight-pointed Star

 3034. Aunt Eliza's Star

The Locked Star 3029. The Locked Star

 3035. Variable Star

 3030. Eight Hand Round

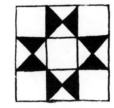 3036. Shoofly*

 3031. Christmas Star

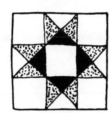 3037. Variable Star

 3032. Claws

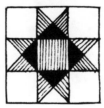 3038. Variable Star†

* *Also:* Texas Star, Ohio Star, Lucky Star, Tippecanoe and Tyler, too, Lone Star, Eastern Star, Eight-point Star, Star, Variable Star, Eight-point Designs, California Star.
† *Also:* Ohio Star.

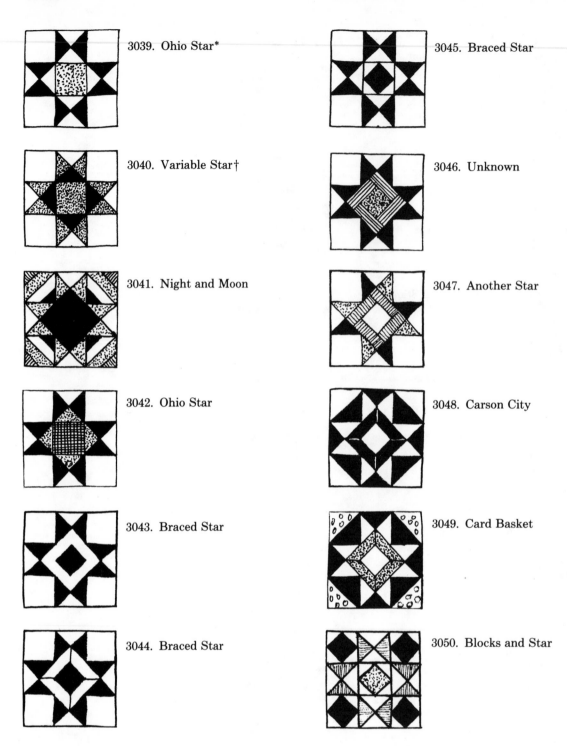

3039. Ohio Star*

3045. Braced Star

3040. Variable Star†

3046. Unknown

3041. Night and Moon

3047. Another Star

3042. Ohio Star

3048. Carson City

3043. Braced Star

3049. Card Basket

3044. Braced Star

3050. Blocks and Star

* *Also:* Variable Star, Ohio.
† *Also:* Ohio Star.

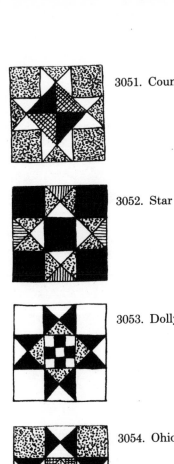 3051. Country Farm

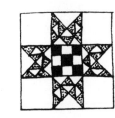 3057. Dolly Madison Star

3052. Star

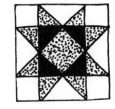 3058. Dolly Madison's Star

3053. Dolly Madison's Star

 3059. Ohio Star

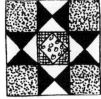 3054. Ohio Star

 3060. Old Tippecanoe

 3055. Dolly Madison*

 3061. The Cog Block

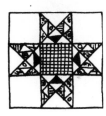 3056. The Kaleidoscope Quilt

 3062. Crystal Star

* *Also:* Santa Fe, Dolly Madison Star.

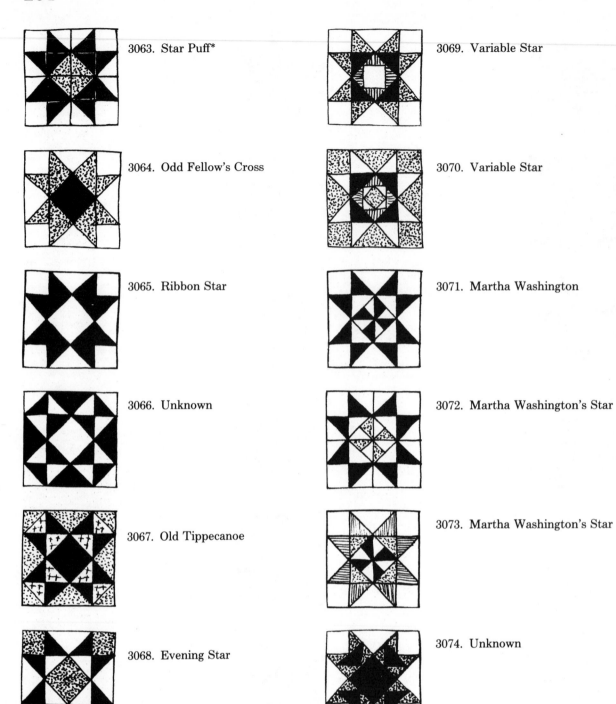

3063. Star Puff*

3064. Odd Fellow's Cross

3065. Ribbon Star

3066. Unknown

3067. Old Tippecanoe

3068. Evening Star

3069. Variable Star

3070. Variable Star

3071. Martha Washington

3072. Martha Washington's Star

3073. Martha Washington's Star

3074. Unknown

*Also: Lone Star.

 3075. Northumberland Star

 3076. Sawtooth and Star

 3077. Joseph's Coat

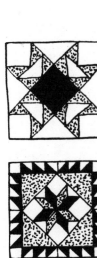 3078. Northumberland Star

 3079. Star of Many Points

 3080. Unknown

 3081. Unknown

 3082. Virginia Star

 3083. Eastern Star*

 3084. Blazing Star

 3085. Eastern Star

 3086. Blazing Star

* *Also:* Little Stars of Bethlehem, Little Stars.

3087. Star of the Bluegrass

3093. Blazing Star

3088. Unknown

3094. Star of Bethlehem*

3089. Northwest Star

3095. Prairie Star†

3090. Northwest Star

3096. Harvest Sun‡

3091. Blazing Star

3097. Unknown

3092. Blazing Star

3098. Ship's Wheel

* *Also:* Patty's Star.
† *Also:* Harvest Sun, Ship's Wheel.
‡ *Also:* Star of Bethlehem, Lone Star, Star of the West, Rising Sun.

3099. Star of Bethlehem

3100. Virginia Star

3101. Harvest Sun

3102. West Virginia Star

3103. Stars of Alabama*

3104. Blazing Stars

    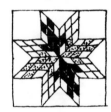 

3105. Giant Star

3106. Virginia Star

3107. Rising Sun

3108. Formosa Tea Leaf

3109. Four Doves in a Window

3110. Flying Bats

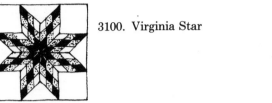

* *Also:* Star of the Bluegrass, Virginia Star.

 3111. Dove in the Window

 3117. The Lone Star

 3112. Dove in the Window

 3118. Eight-point Star

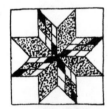 3113. Inlay Star

 3119. Rainbow Star

 3114. Formosa Tea Leaf

 3120. Touching Stars

 3115. Star upon Stars

 3121. Feathered Star

 3116. Star of Bethlehem

 3122. Feathered Star

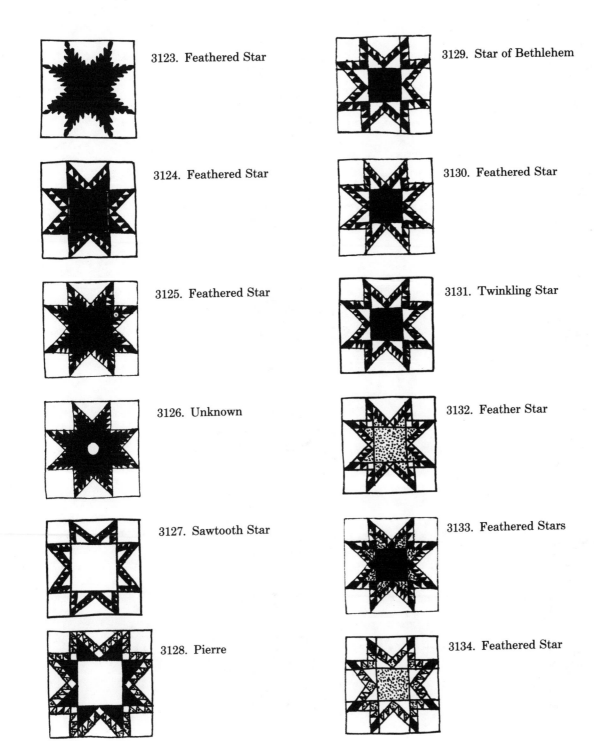

3123. Feathered Star

3124. Feathered Star

3125. Feathered Star

3126. Unknown

3127. Sawtooth Star

3128. Pierre

3129. Star of Bethlehem

3130. Feathered Star

3131. Twinkling Star

3132. Feather Star

3133. Feathered Stars

3134. Feathered Star

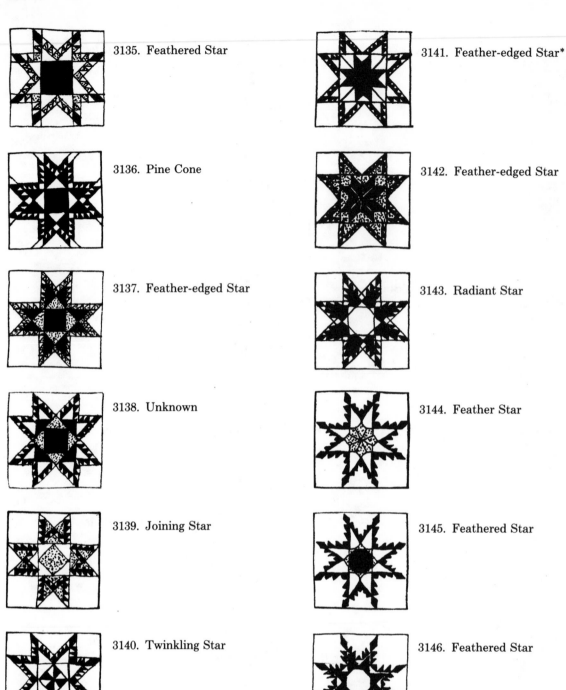

3135. Feathered Star

3136. Pine Cone

3137. Feather-edged Star

3138. Unknown

3139. Joining Star

3140. Twinkling Star

3141. Feather-edged Star*

3142. Feather-edged Star

3143. Radiant Star

3144. Feather Star

3145. Feathered Star

3146. Feathered Star

* *Also:* Feathered Star.

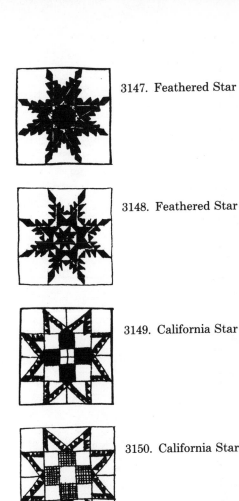 3147. Feathered Star

3148. Feathered Star

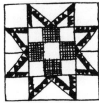 3149. California Star

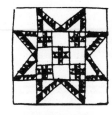 3150. California Star

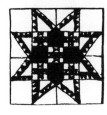 3151. California Star

3152. California Star

 3153. California Star

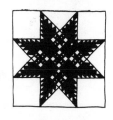 3154. California Star

 3155. Star-spangled Banner

 3156. French Star

 3157. French Star

 3158. Biloxi

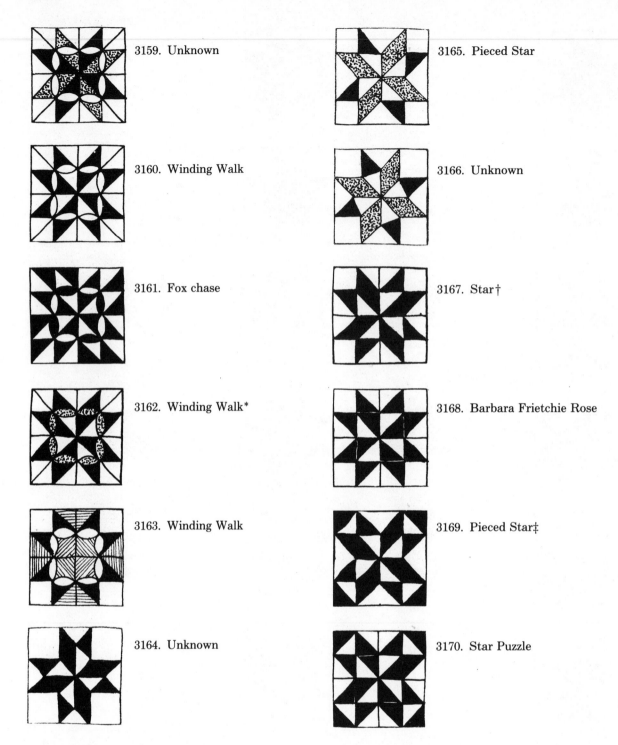

3159. Unknown

3160. Winding Walk

3161. Fox chase

3162. Winding Walk*

3163. Winding Walk

3164. Unknown

3165. Pieced Star

3166. Unknown

3167. Star†

3168. Barbara Frietchie Rose

3169. Pieced Star‡

3170. Star Puzzle

* *Also:* Fox Chase.
† *Also:* Barbara Frietchie's Design.
‡ *also:* Barbara Frietchie Star.

 3171. Star Puzzle

 3177. Pieced Star

 3172. Pieced Star

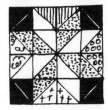 3178. Quilter's Surprise

 3173. Barbara Frietchie's Star

 3179. Mother's Favorite Star

 3174. Star Puzzle

 3180. Rolling Star *

 3175. Summer Star

 3181. Unknown

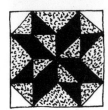 3176. Unknown

 3182. Rolling Star

* *Also* Eight-pointed Star.

274

 3183. Brunswick Star

 3189. Unknown

 3184. St. Louis Block

 3190. Double Star†

3185. Rolling Stone

 3191. Unknown

3186. Windmill

 3192. Stars and Cubes

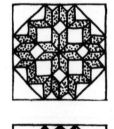 3187. Dutch Rose*

3193. A Flash of Diamonds

3188. Star of the East

 3194. LeMoyne Star

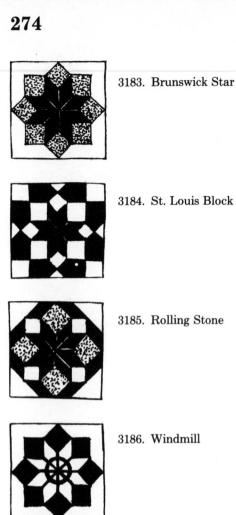

* *Also:* Octagonal Star, Broken Star.
† *Also:* Double Rose, Broken Star.

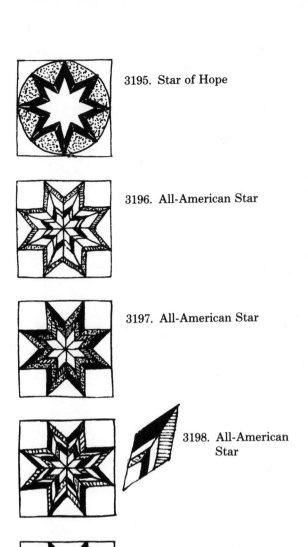

3195. Star of Hope

3196. All-American Star

3197. All-American Star

3198. All-American Star

3199. Helena*

3200. Star of Stripes

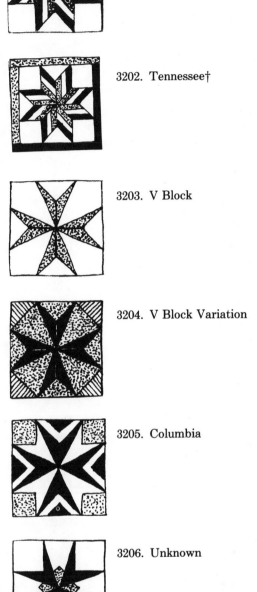

3201. Liberty Star

3202. Tennessee†

3203. V Block

3204. V Block Variation

3205. Columbia

3206. Unknown

* *Also:* Spiderweb.
† *Also:* Liberty Star, Star of Bethlehem.

3207. St. Louis

3213. Unknown

3208. St. Louis Star

3214. Star of North Carolina

3209. St. Louis Star Variation

3215. Star of North Carolina

3210. Missouri Star

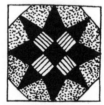

3216. Unknown

3211. Unknown

3217. Morning Star

3212. Unknown

3218. North Carolina

 3219. Star and Cross

 3225. Starlight

 3220. Mexican Cross

 3226. Starlight

 3221. Mexican Star

 3227. Starlight

 3222. Rolling Star

 3228. The Arkansas Star

 3223. Star and Chains

 3229. Unknown

 3224. Eight-pointed Star

 3230. St. Louis Star

3231. Enigma Star

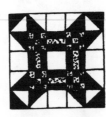

3237. Missouri Puzzle

3232. St. Louis Block

3238. Missouri Puzzle

3233. St. Louis Star

3239. Rolling Pinwheel

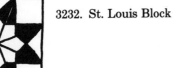

3234. St. Louis Block

3240. Pinwheel Star

3235. Family Affection

3241. Flying Swallows

3236. New Mexico

3242. Flying Swallow*

* *Also:* Flying Barn Swallow.

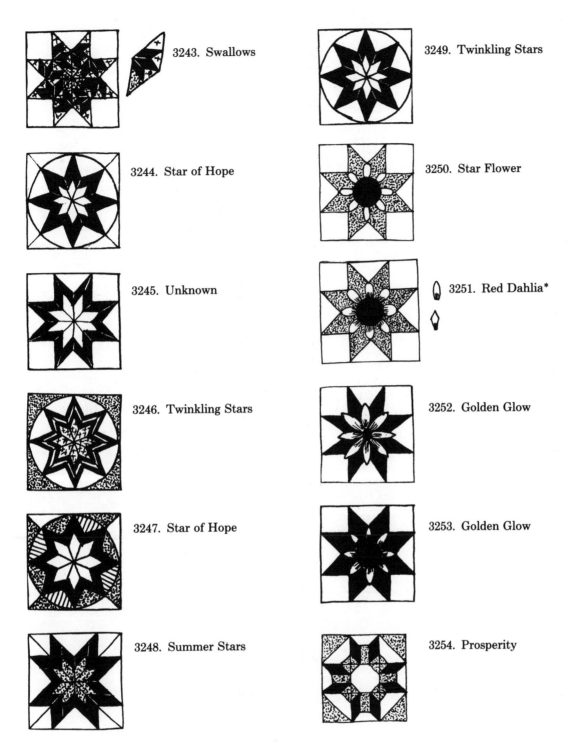

3243. Swallows

3249. Twinkling Stars

3244. Star of Hope

3250. Star Flower

3245. Unknown

3251. Red Dahlia*

3246. Twinkling Stars

3252. Golden Glow

3247. Star of Hope

3253. Golden Glow

3248. Summer Stars

3254. Prosperity

* *Also:* Golden Glow, Missouri Daisy, Three-dimensional Dahlia, Dahlia.

 3255. Prosperity

 3261. Springfield

 3256. Castle Wall

 3262. Grandmother's Choice

 3257. Castle Wall

 3263. Springfield

 3258. Castle Wall

 3264. Grandmother's Choice

 3259. String Star

 3265. Unknown

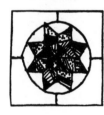 3260. Log Cabin Star

 3266. Shadow Star

 3267. Shadow Star

 3268. End of Summer Star

 3269. Tennessee Star

 3270. Dahlia

 3271. Shadow Star

 3272. Star and Crown

 3273. Pieced Morning Glory

 3274. Tennessee Star

 3275. Silver and Gold

 3276. Skyrocket

 3277. Skyrocket

 3278. Skyrocket

3279. Double Diamond

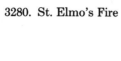

3280. St. Elmo's Fire

3281. Unknown

3282. Unknown

3283. Stepping-stones

3284. Black Beauty

3285. No-name Quilt

3286. Unknown

3287. Sunburst

3288. Unknown

3289. Harrisburg

3290. Eight-pointed Star

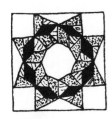 3291. Flying Swallows

 3297. Stars and Stripes

 3292. Missouri

 3298. Farmer's Daughter

 3293. Indianapolis

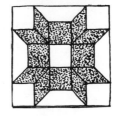 3299. Flying Saucer

 3294. Bull's-eye

 3300. Lucinda's Star

 3295. Weathervane

 3301. Farmer's Wife

 3296. Star of Many Points

 3302. Compass and Star

 3303. The Little Giant

 3309. Enigma Star

 3304. Unknown

 3310. Columbian Star

 3305. Hope of Hartford

 3311. Jupiter Star

 3306. Grandma's Star and Web

 3312. Evening Star

 3307. Jan's Bicentennial Star

 3313. Lazy Daisy

 3308. Falling Star

 3314. Farmer's Wife

 3315. Unknown

 3321. Nine-patch Star

 3316. T Blocks

 3322. Sitka

 3317. Triple Irish Chain and Eight-point Star

 3323. The Long-pointed Star

 3318. Unknown

 3324. Star and Cone

 3319. North Star

 3325. Starry Path

 3320. New Star

 3326. Triple Star

 3327. Unknown

 3333. Star and Chains

 3328. Broken Crystals

 3334. All Hallows

 3329. Wandering Diamond

 3335. St. Louis Star

 3330. Royal Star Quilt

 3336. Diamond Star

 3331. Lucinda's Star

 3337. Budding Star

 3332. Unknown Star

 3338. Pinwheel Star

 3339. Brunswick Star

 3345. Delectable Mountains

 3340. St. Louis Star

 3346. Morning Star

 3341. Little Giant

 3347. Evening Star

 3342. Unknown

 3348. Grandma's Surprise

 3343. The Old Spanish Tile Pattern

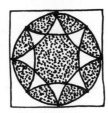 3349. The Car Wheel Quilt

 3344. Unknown

 3350. Rhode Island

3351. Stepping-stones

3352. Star Bright

3353. Unknown

3354. Starry Heavens

3355. Unknown

3356. Water Lily

3357. Unknown

3358. Album Quilt

3359. Album Quilt (pieced and appliquéd)

3360. Odd Fellow's Chain

3361. Odd Fellow's Chain

3362. Georgetown Circle

 3363. Safari

 3369. Sand Hills Star

 3364. Unknown

 3370. Kansas Star

 3365. Diamond Star

 3371. Kansas

 3366. Dove at the Window

 3372. The Double-star Quilt

 3367. Unknown

 3373. Unknown

 3368. Star of Many Points

 3374. Bethlehem Star

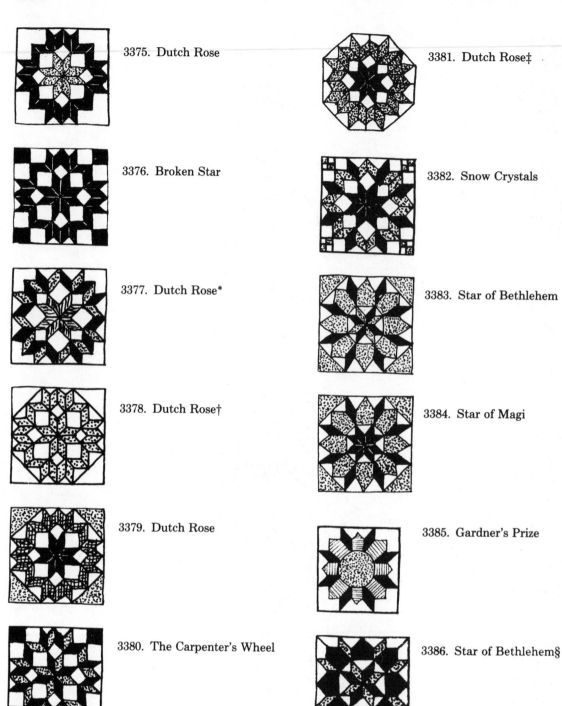

3375. Dutch Rose

3381. Dutch Rose‡

3376. Broken Star

3382. Snow Crystals

3377. Dutch Rose*

3383. Star of Bethlehem

3378. Dutch Rose†

3384. Star of Magi

3379. Dutch Rose

3385. Gardner's Prize

3380. The Carpenter's Wheel

3386. Star of Bethlehem§

* *Also:* Star with Diamonds.
† *Also:* Octagonal Star, Broken Star.
‡ *Also:* Octagonal Star.
§ *Also:* Star of Jerusalem.

 3387. Star of Bethlehem

 3393. Sunburst

 3388. My Nova

 3394. Slashed Star

 3389. The Lone Star of Paradise

 3395. Chips and Whetstones

 3390. Unknown

 3396. Unknown

 3391. Man in the Moon

 3397. Blazing Star*

 3392. Wyoming

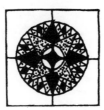 3398. Compass

* *Also:* Blazing Sun.

 3399. Sunflower*

 3405. Mariner's Compass

 3400. Sunburst

 3406. Mariner's Compass

 3401. Mariner's Compass

 3407. Slashed Star

 3402. Unknown

 3408. Chips and Whetstones

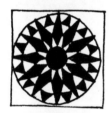 3403. Sunburst†

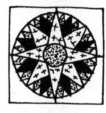 3409. Compass

 3404. Sunburst

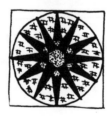 3410. Mariner's Compass

* *Also:* Blazing Sun, Blazing Star.
† *Also:* Mariner's Compass, Sunflower, Rolling Pinwheel.

 3411. Georgetown Circle

 3417. Explosion

 3412. Mariner's Compass

 3418. Chips and Whetstones

 3413. Mariner's Compass

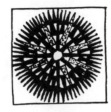 3419. Mariner's Compass

 3414. Mariner's Compass

 3420. Sunburst

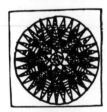 3415. Mariner's Compass

 3421. Sunburst

 3416. Mariner's Compass

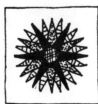 3422. Unknown

 3423. Mariner's Compass

 3429. Sunburst

 3424. Chips and Whetstones

 3430. Sunburst

 3425. Mariner's Compass

 3431. Sunburst

 3426. Slashed Star

 3432. Russian Sunflower

 3427. Mariner's Compass

 3433. Unknown

 3428. Unknown

 3434. Single Sunflower

 3435. Russian Sunflower

 3441. Dresden Plate

 3436. Sunflower

 3442. Sunburst

 3437. Chrysanthemum

 3443. Mariner's Compass

 3438. Unknown

 3444. Aurora Borealis*

 3439. Dresden Plate

 3445. Unknown

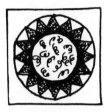 3440. Oklahoma Sunburst

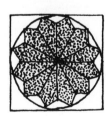 3446. The Buzz Saw

* *Also:* Northern Star.

3447. Unknown

3453. Friendship Knot

3448. Unknown

3454. Hands All Around

3449. Unknown

3455. All Hands Round

3450. Mariner's Compass

3456. Hands All Around

3451. Mariner's Compass

3457. Hands All Around

3452. Sunburst in a Garden Maze

3458. Unknown

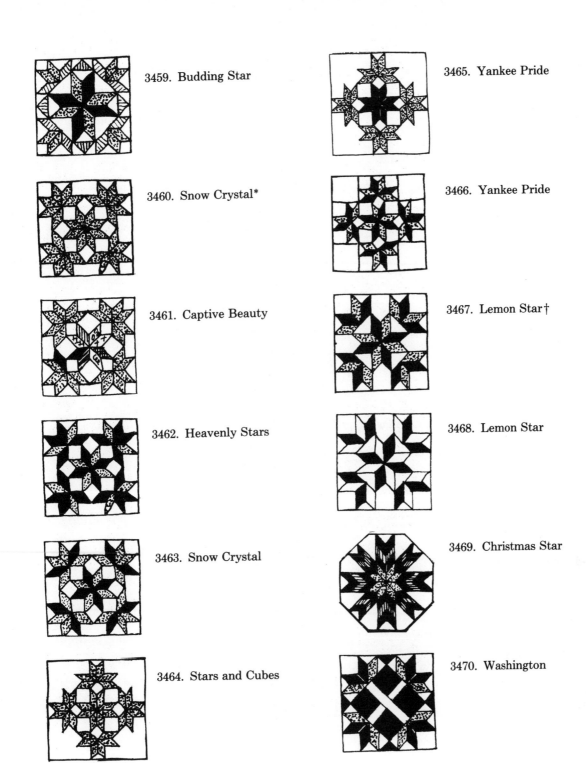

3459. Budding Star

3465. Yankee Pride

3460. Snow Crystal*

3466. Yankee Pride

3461. Captive Beauty

3467. Lemon Star†

3462. Heavenly Stars

3468. Lemon Star

3463. Snow Crystal

3469. Christmas Star

3464. Stars and Cubes

3470. Washington

* *Also:* Dove at My Window.
† *Also:* LeMoyne Star.

 3471. Hartford

 3477. Jackson Star

 3472. Square and Star

 3478. Spinning Triangles

 3473. Unknown

 3479. Sunburst

 3474. Star of North Carolina

 3480. Unknown

 3475. Unknown

 3481. Modern Star

 3476. Royal Star (pieced and appliquéd)

 3482. Alice's Favorite

 3483. Prairie Queen

 3489. Snowball

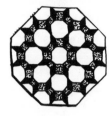 3484. Unknown

 3490. Star

 3485. Unknown Star

 3491. Golden Wedding*

 3486. Unknown

 3492. North Dakota

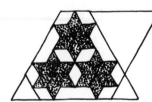 3487. The Triple Star

 3493. Diamond Star

 3488. Periwinkle

 3494. Kaleidoscope

* *Also:* World without End.

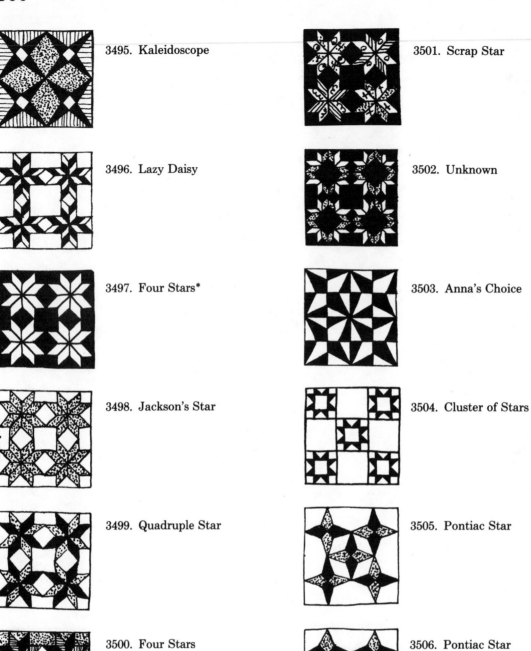

3495. Kaleidoscope

3496. Lazy Daisy

3497. Four Stars*

3498. Jackson's Star

3499. Quadruple Star

3500. Four Stars

3501. Scrap Star

3502. Unknown

3503. Anna's Choice

3504. Cluster of Stars

3505. Pontiac Star

3506. Pontiac Star

* *Also:* Jackson's Star.

 3507. Unknown

 3511. Seven Stars

 3508. Hollywood

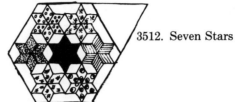 3512. Seven Stars

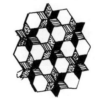

 3509. Stars and Blocks*

3513. Star and Hexagon

 3510. Hexagon Star

* *Also:* Tumbling Blocks, Columbian Star.

Overall Patterns

One basic piece used repeatedly
to form pattern

Patterns 3514 to 3741

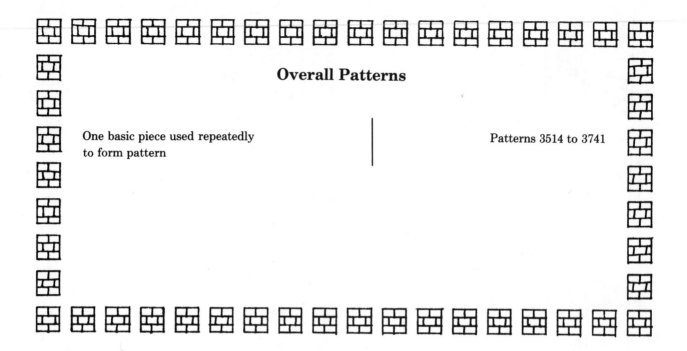

3514. Streak o' Lightning

3515. Bricks*

3516. Streak o' Lightning

3517. Aunt Sukey's Patch

3518. Hit or Miss

3519. Hit or Miss

* *Also:* Brick Wall.

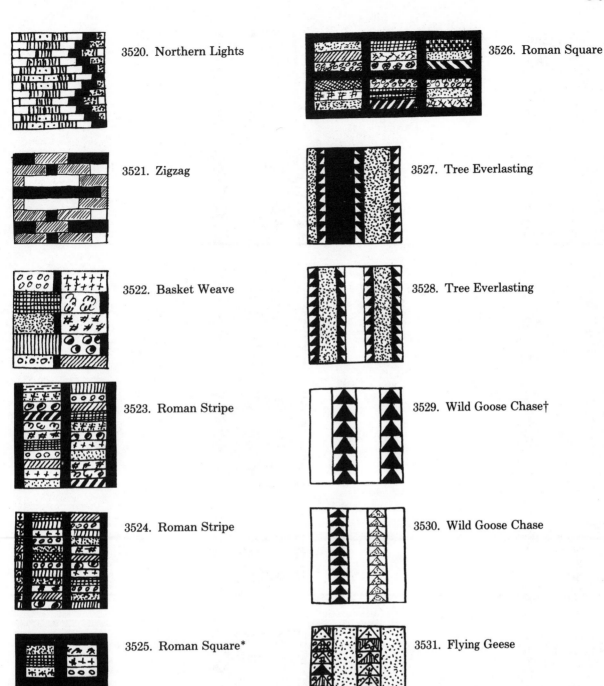

3520. Northern Lights

3521. Zigzag

3522. Basket Weave

3523. Roman Stripe

3524. Roman Stripe

3525. Roman Square*

3526. Roman Square

3527. Tree Everlasting

3528. Tree Everlasting

3529. Wild Goose Chase†

3530. Wild Goose Chase

3531. Flying Geese

* *Also:* Roman Block.
† *Also:* Flying Geese, Birds in Flight.

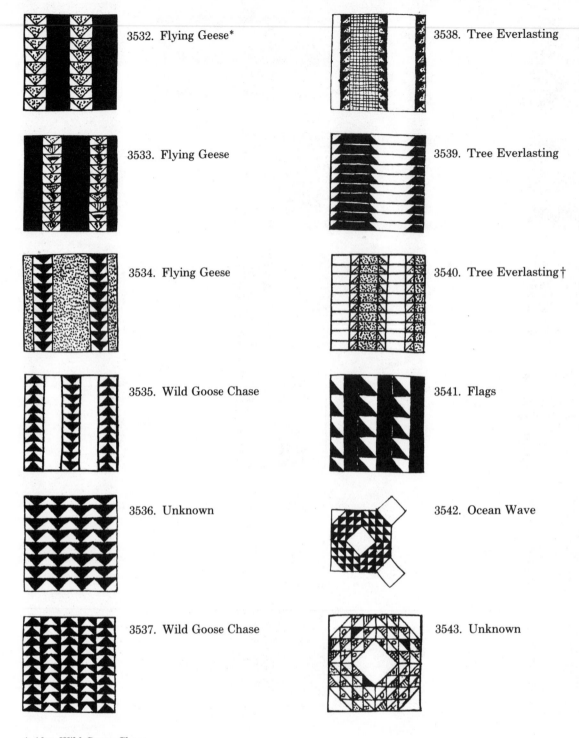

3532. Flying Geese*

3533. Flying Geese

3534. Flying Geese

3535. Wild Goose Chase

3536. Unknown

3537. Wild Goose Chase

3538. Tree Everlasting

3539. Tree Everlasting

3540. Tree Everlasting†

3541. Flags

3542. Ocean Wave

3543. Unknown

* *Also:* Wild Goose Chase.
† *Also:* Herringbone, Prickly Path, The Path of Thorns, Arrowheads.

 3544. Ocean Wave

 3550. Sea Shell

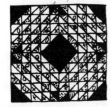 3545. Ocean Waves

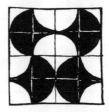 3551. Spanish Grillwork

 3546. Shell Chain*

 3552. Clamshell

 3547. Clamshell

 3553. Rail Fence

 3548. Clamshell

 3554. Coarse-woven Patch

 3549. Clamshell

 3555. Fine-woven Patchwork

* *Also:* Clamshell.

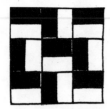 3556. London Stairs

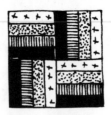 3562. Rail Fence

 3557. Basket Weave

 3563. Rail Fence

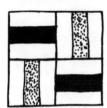 3558. Roman Stripe*

 3564. Roman Square†

 3559. Rail Fence

 3565. Roman Square‡

 3560. Roman Square

 3566. Rail Fence

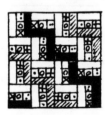 3561. Autumn Rail Fence

 3567. Country Charm

Also: Zigzag.
†*Also:* Roman Block.
‡*Also:* Roman Block.

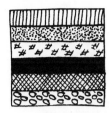 3568. Roman Stripe

 3569. Five Stripes

 3570. Unknown

 3571. Tumbler

 3572. Tumbler

 3573. Tumbler

 3574. Tumbler

 3575. Patience Corners

 3576. Ribbons

 3577. Zigzag

 3578. Ecclesiastic

 3579. Inner City

3580. Ecclesiastical

3581. Crazy Quilt (may be in squares, stripes, alternating with plain block, overall)

3582. Crazy Patch

3583. Diamond Crazy Quilt

3584. Crazy Quilt

3585. Charm Quilt

3586. Spools

3587. Friendship*

3588. Honeycomb

3589. Honeycomb

3590. Honeycomb

3591. Lightning

* *Also:* Spool, Friendship Quilt, Always Friends, Friendship Chain, Apple Core, Double Ax Head, Rail Fence.

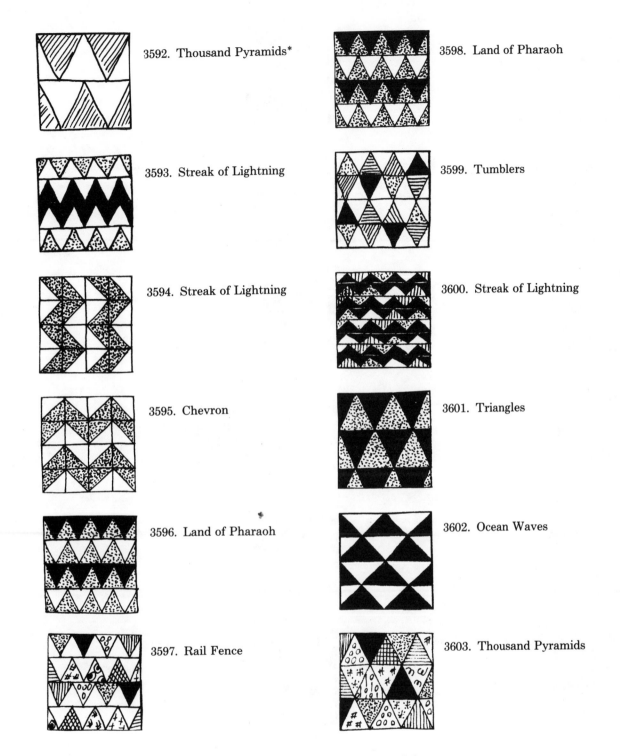

3592. Thousand Pyramids*

3598. Land of Pharaoh

3593. Streak of Lightning

3599. Tumblers

3594. Streak of Lightning

3600. Streak of Lightning

3595. Chevron

3601. Triangles

3596. Land of Pharaoh

3602. Ocean Waves

3597. Rail Fence

3603. Thousand Pyramids

* *Also:* Streak of Lightning, Zigzag, Rail Fence, Snake Fence, Triangles All Over.

3604. Pyramids

3605. Unknown

3606. Slashed Diagonal

3607. Broken Dishes

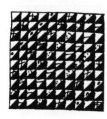

3608. Ocean Wave

3609. Diagonal Triangles

3610. Windmills

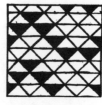

3611. The Wild Goose Quilt

3612. Illusion

3613. Variable Triangles

3614. Twist Patchwork

3615. Patriot's Quilt

3616. Tile Puzzle

3622. Pandora's Box

3617. Puzzle Tile

3623. Brick Pile

3618. The Twist

3624. Pandora's Box

3619. Round the Twist

3625. Baby's Blocks Variation

3620. Octagonal Tile*

3626. Baby's Blocks†

3621. Grandmother's Dream

3627. Baby's Blocks

* *Also:* Grandmother's Dream.
† *Also:* Diamond Cube, Cube Work, Magic Cubes, Boxes, Tumbling Blocks, Grandma's Red and White, Stairway to Paradise, Box Quilt, Baby Blocks, Pandora's Box.

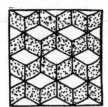 3628. Variegated Diamonds

 3634. Heritage Quilt

 3629. Grandma's Red and White

 3635. Streak of Lightning

 3630. Diamond Design

 3636. Ford's Quilt

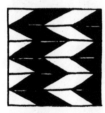 3631. Zigzag*

 3637. Diamond

 3632. Chevron

 3638. Diamonds

 3633. Unknown

 3639. Diamonds

* *Also:* Lightning.

 3640. Walk Around*

 3646. Floating Star (four blocks shown)

3641. Red, White, and Blue Diamonds

 3647. Boston Corners

3642. Diamonds (4-inch pieces)

 3648. Checkerboard

3643. Unknown

 3649. Unknown

3644. Shadow Trail

 3650. Postage Stamp

3645. The Xquisite

 3651. Hit or Miss†

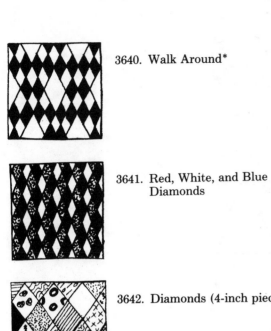

* *Also:* Boston Corners.
† *Also:* Hairpin Catcha.

3652. Streak of Lightning

3658. Triple Irish Chain

3653. Nine-patch

3659. Glorified Irish Chain

3654. Friendship Square

3660. Cross-patch

3655. Diamond Arrangement

3661. Checkerboard Paths

3656. Unknown

3662. Cable Blocks

3657. Improved Nine-patch

3663. Mosaic

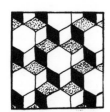 3664. No Name

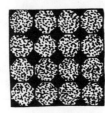 3670. Diamond and Star*

 3665. Hexagon Puff

 3671. Octagons

 3666. Bow Tie

 3672. Ozark Cobblestones

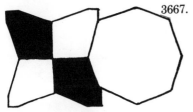 3667. The Periwinkle

 3673. Unknown

 3668. Red and Blue Octagon

 3674. Honeycomb Patchwork

 3669. World without End

 3675. Honeycomb

* *Also:* World without End.

3676. Stained Glass

3677. Fantastic Patchwork

3678. Lover's Links

3679. Attic Windows (cut on bias)

3680. Attic Windows

3681. Unknown

3682. Magic Squares

3683. Puffed Quilt*

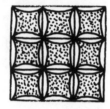

3684. Pin Cushion

3685. Bay Leaf (can be large or small)

3686. Arabic Lattice

3687. Arabic Lattice

* *Also:* Biscuit, Bun.

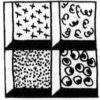

3688. Irish Chain

3694. Unknown

3689. Irish Chain Variation

3695. Crisscross*

3690. Triple Irish Chain

3696. Oklahoma String Quilt

3691. The Kansas Dugout

3697. Godey's Lady Quilt

3692. Unknown

3698. Rob Peter, Pay Paul†

3693. Unknown

3699. Steeplechase

* *Also:* Patchwork.
† *Also:* Lend and Borrow.

3700. Roman Stripe

3701. Zigzag

3702. Chevron

3703. Tile Patchwork

3704. Chinese Puzzle

3705. Four-leaf Clover

3706. Flying Bats

3707. Tallahassee Quilt

3708. Cube Lattice

3709. Bow Knots

3710. Ice Cream Cone

3711. Indian Chief (stagger blocks when joining)

 3712. Grandma's Favorite

 3718. Pinwheel

 3713. Complex T

 3719. Chain of Diamonds

 3714. Lilies of the Field

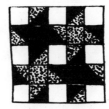 3720. Milky Way

 3715. Spanish Tiles

 3721. Basket Lattice

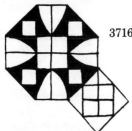 3716. Crusader's Cross

 3722. Weaving Paths

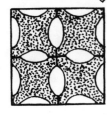 3717. Compass*

 3723. Road to Oklahoma

* *Also:* Orange Peel.

3724. Road to Oklahoma

3730. Unknown

3725. Four-patch

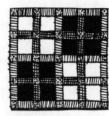

3731. Unknown

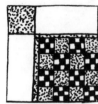

3726. Nine-patch (one-quarter quilt shown)

3732. Cupid's Arrow Point

3727. Circle Nine-patch

3733. Cupid's Arrow Point

3728. Squares in Squares

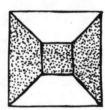

3734. Spools

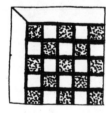

3729. Checkerboard (one-quarter quilt shown)

3735. Chain and Hourglass

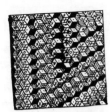 3736. Stairway to Heaven (all pieces are diamonds)

 3737. Unknown

 3738. Checkerboard Quilt

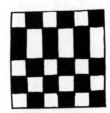 3739. Unknown

 3740. Honeycomb

 3741. Spiderweb

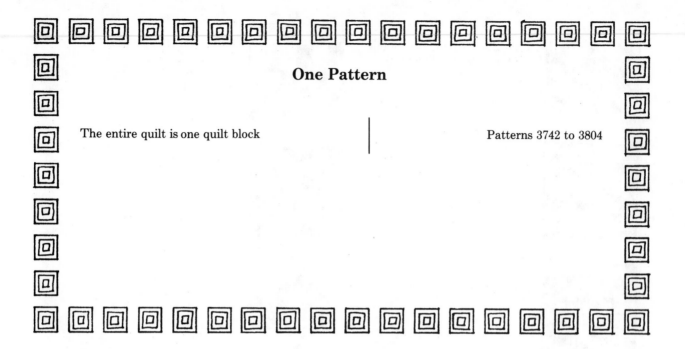

One Pattern

The entire quilt is one quilt block

Patterns 3742 to 3804

3742. Royal Aster (shades of one color)

3745. Solomon's Temple

3743. The Giant Dahlia

3746. Delectable Mountains

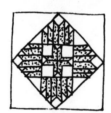

3744. Rising Sun

3747. Solomon's Temple

3748. Delectable Mountains

3754. Unknown

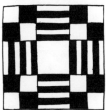

3749. Unknown

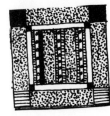

3755. Amish Stripes and Squares

3750. Star within a Star

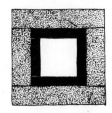

3756. Center Square

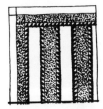

3751. Tree Everlasting

3757. Bars (one-quarter quilt shown)

3752. Bars

3758. Unknown (1-inch bands)

3753. Bars

3759. Rainbow

3760. Bars

3766. The Reversible Novel

3761. Split Bars

3767. Center Diamond

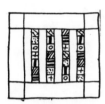

3762. Bars (all solid colors)

3768. Sawtooth

3763. Bars

3769. Unknown

3764. Barn Raising

3770. Center Diamond

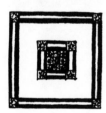

3765. Morning Glory's Stars and Stripes

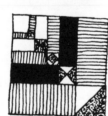

3771. Unknown

 3772. Unknown

 3778. Stars and Blocks

 3773. Amish Diamond Quilt

 3779. Lone Star Variation (one-quarter quilt shown)

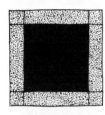 3774. Center Square

 3780. Mosaic Star

 3775. Center Square

 3781. Lone Star†

 3776. Center Diamond*

 3782. Lone Star

 3777. Sunburst

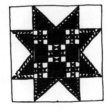 3783. Large Feathered Star

* *Also:* Diamond Quilt.
† *Also:* Star of Bethlehem, Rising Star, Texas Star.

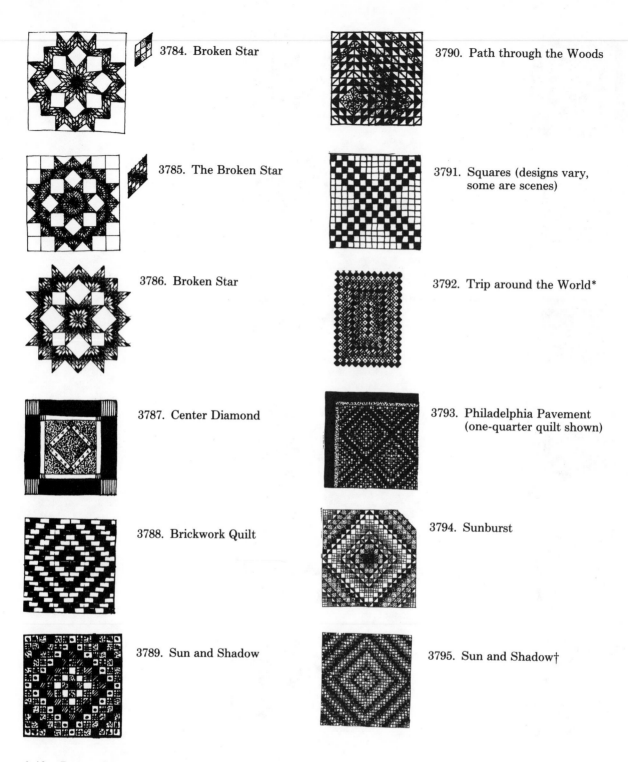

3784. Broken Star

3785. The Broken Star

3786. Broken Star

3787. Center Diamond

3788. Brickwork Quilt

3789. Sun and Shadow

3790. Path through the Woods

3791. Squares (designs vary, some are scenes)

3792. Trip around the World*

3793. Philadelphia Pavement (one-quarter quilt shown)

3794. Sunburst

3795. Sun and Shadow†

* *Also:* Postage Stamp.
† *Also:* Trip around the World, Crossword Puzzle, Checkerboard, Philadelphia Pavement.

 3796. Sunburst *

 3801. Sunshine and Shadow

 3797. The Lincoln Quilt

 3802. Square-in-square

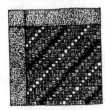 3798. Amish Diagonal † (all plain colors: one-quarter quilt shown)

 3803. Sunshine and Shadow‡

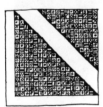 3799. Square in a Square (one-quarter quilt shown)

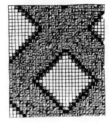 3804. Quilt of a Thousand Pieces§

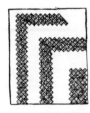 3800. Boston Commons (one-quarter quilt shown)

* *Also:* Rising Sun.
† *Also:* Sunshine and Shadow.
‡ *Also:* Crossword Puzzle.
§*Also:* Postage Stamp.

Other Patterns

Patterns that do not fit in any other category

Patterns 3805 to 4002

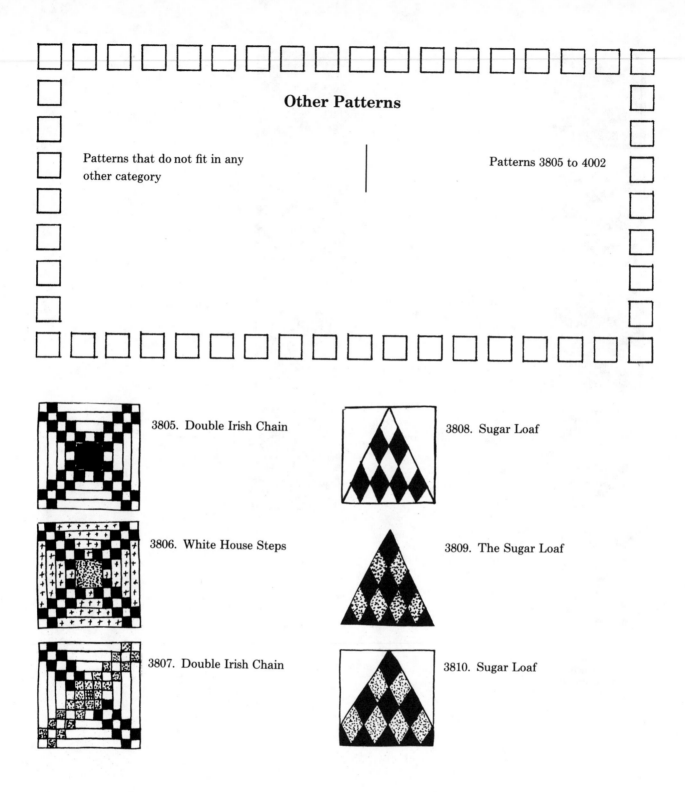

3805. Double Irish Chain

3808. Sugar Loaf

3806. White House Steps

3809. The Sugar Loaf

3807. Double Irish Chain

3810. Sugar Loaf

 3811. Triangular Triangle

 3817. Ice Cream Bowl

 3812. Triangle Quilt

 3818. Sawtooth Strips

 3813. Triangular Triangles

 3819. Star Flower

 3814. Charm

 3820. Sawtooth

 3815. Unknown

 3821. Washington's Puzzle

 3816. Ice Cream Bowl

 3822. Checkerboard Skew

 3823. Triangle Puzzle

 3829. Washington's Quilt

 3824. Poinsettia

 3830. Chimney Swallows

 3825. Friendship Knot

 3831. Coronation*

 3826. Grandmother's Wedding Quilt

 3832. Chimney Swallows

 3827. Whigs Defeat

 3833. Coronation 1830†

 3828. Chimney Swallows

 3834. Stephen A. Douglas

* *Also:* King's Crown, President's Quilt, Potomac Pride.
† *Also:* King's Crown, Coronation, President's Quilt, Washington's Potomac Pride.

 3835. Little Giant

 3841. California

 3836. The Little Giant

 3842. California

3837. Heart's Desire

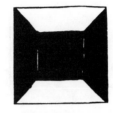 3843. Spool Quilt

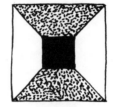 3838. Crow's-foot

 3844. Spool

 3839. Crow-foot

 3845. Bat Wings

3840. Stained Glass

 3846. Bat Wings

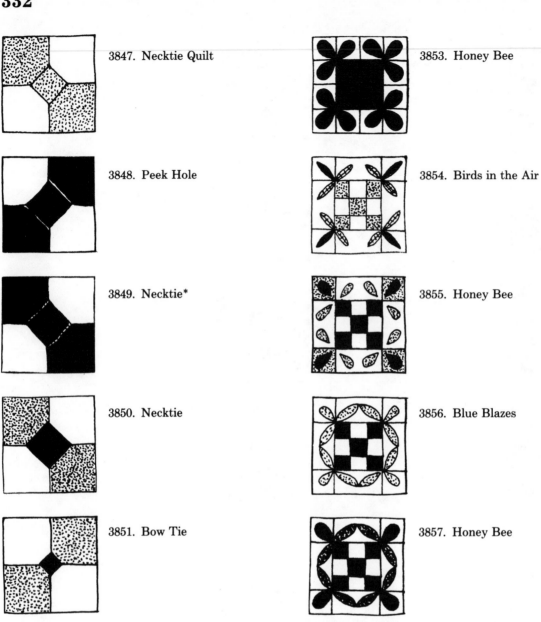

3847. Necktie Quilt

3848. Peek Hole

3849. Necktie*

3850. Necktie

3851. Bow Tie

3852. Turkey Track (pieced and appliquéd)

3853. Honey Bee

3854. Birds in the Air

3855. Honey Bee

3856. Blue Blazes

3857. Honey Bee

3858. Unknown

* *Also:* Bow Tie.

 3859. Unknown

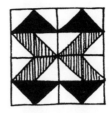 3865. Brown Goose

 3860. Mosaic

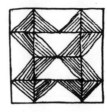 3866. Brown Goose†

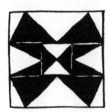 3861. Double Z*

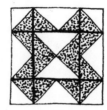 3867. Brown Goose

 3862. Bow Tie

 3868. Hourglass

 3863. Bow

 3869. Double Z‡

 3864. Double Z

 3870. Hawaii

* *Also:* Gray Goose.
† *Also:* Gray Goose, Devil's Claws, Double Z.
‡ *Also:* Brown Goose.

3871. Miss Jackson

3872. Jackson

3873. Unknown

3874. Unknown

3875. Save All

3876. Save All

3877. An Odd Patchwork

3878. Burgoyne Surrounded

3879. Burgoyne Quilt*

3880. Odd Patchwork

3881. Madam X

3882. Neil's Diamond

* *Also:* Burgoyne Surrounded, Homestead, Wheel of Fortune, The Road to California, Homespun.

3883. Bridal Stairway*

3884. Crazy Quilt

3885. Diamond Nine-patch†

3886. Ocean Waves

3887. Ocean Waves

3888. Old Mexico

3889. Grandmother's Cross

3890. Hexagon Star

3891. Long Hexagon

3892. Peddler

3893. Cube Work‡

3894. Rail Fence

* *Also:* Bridal Path.
† *Also:* Nine-patch Diamond.
‡ *Also:* Baby's Block.

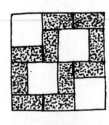 3895. Patience Corner

 3901. Alabama

 3896. Hayes' Corner

 3902. Flowing Ribbon

 3897. Unknown

 3903. The Flowing Ribbon

 3898. Razzle-Dazzle

 3904. Indian Squares

 3899. Unknown

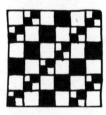 3905. Carrie Nation Quilt

 3900. Square within Squares

 3906. Steps to Glory

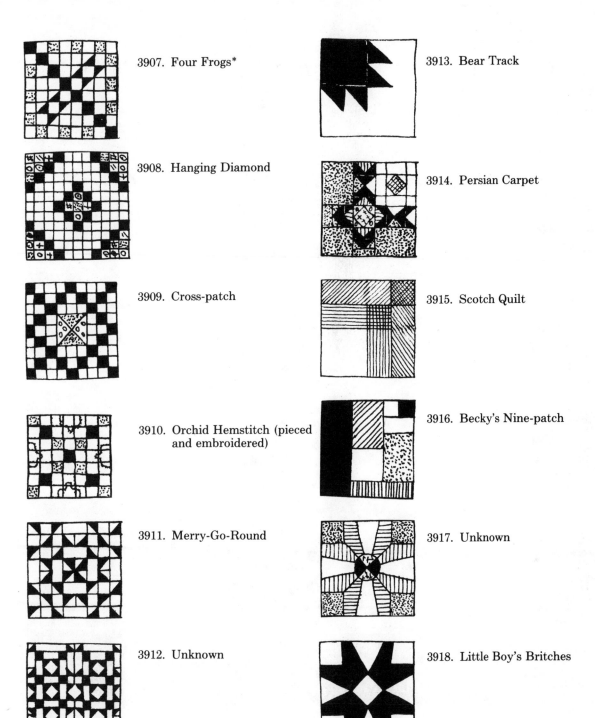

3907. Four Frogs*

3913. Bear Track

3908. Hanging Diamond

3914. Persian Carpet

3909. Cross-patch

3915. Scotch Quilt

3910. Orchid Hemstitch (pieced and embroidered)

3916. Becky's Nine-patch

3911. Merry-Go-Round

3917. Unknown

3912. Unknown

3918. Little Boy's Britches

* *Also:* Flying Clouds.

 3919. Boxed T's

 3925. Farmer's Daughter

 3920. T Quartet

 3926. Fun-time

 3921. Unknown

 3927. Rolling Star

 3922. Serving Set

 3928. Century of Progress

 3923. Wild Goose Chase

 3929. Baton Rouge

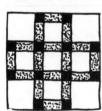 3924. Tick-Tack-Toe

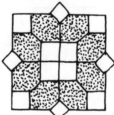 3930. Memory Chain

 3931. Unknown

 3937. Altar Steps

 3932. Unknown

 3938. Full-blown Tulip

 3933. Baton Rouge

 3939. Guthrie

 3934. Eight Diamonds and a Star

 3940. Greek Cross

 3935. Flags and Chevrons

 3941. Quark

 3936. Unknown

 3942. Arkansas Centennial

 3943. Tallahassee

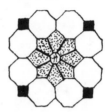 3949. King David's Crown

 3944. Navajo

 3950. Colonial Garden

 3945. Weathervane

 3951. Unknown

 3946. Broken Dishes

 3952. The Winding Blade

 3947. Ceremonial Plaza

 3953. Twisted Ribbon

 3948. Squash Blossom

 3954. Baby Block Variation
(done in strips)

3955. Forget-Me-Not

3961. A Quilt of Variety (four variations shown: basic block)

3956. Walls of Jericho

3962. Unknown

3957. Unknown

3963. Unknown

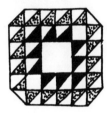

3958. Indian Plume

3964. Meadow Flower

3959. Sawtooth Squares

3965. The Shooting Star

3960. Spiderweb

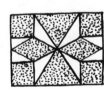

3966. A Butterfly in Angles

 3967. The Farmer's Wife

 3973. String of Beads

 3968. Eccentric Star

 3974. Unknown

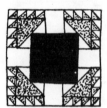 3969. Pine Burr

 3975. Storm at Sea Variation

 3970. Tie Twist

 3976. Dutchman's Delight

 3971. Unknown

 3977. The Goose Track

 3972. Cotton Patch Treasures

 3978. Twist and Turn

 3979. Work Box

 3985. Squares and Stripes

 3980. Unknown

 3986. Unknown

 3981. Unknown

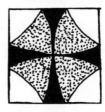 3987. Buttercup

 3982. Shooting Star

 3988. Patchwork Sofa

 3983. Wild Goose Chase

 3989. Ribbon Border Quilt

 3984. Unknown

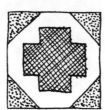 3990. Greek Cross

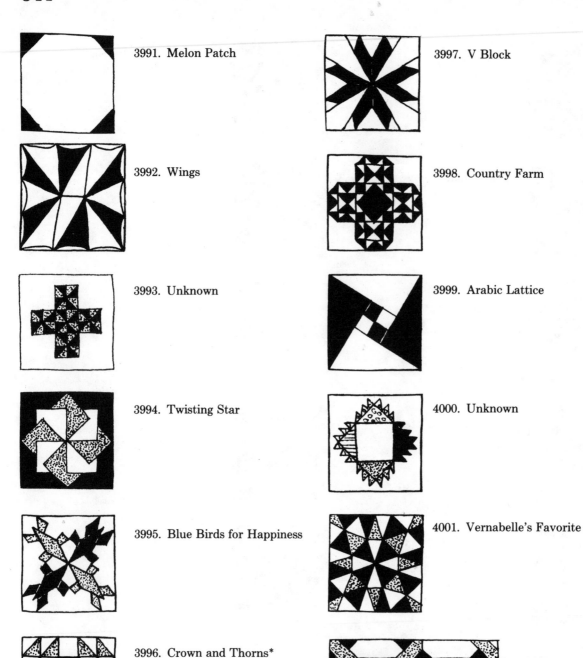

3991. Melon Patch

3997. V Block

3992. Wings

3998. Country Farm

3993. Unknown

3999. Arabic Lattice

3994. Twisting Star

4000. Unknown

3995. Blue Birds for Happiness

4001. Vernabelle's Favorite

3996. Crown and Thorns*

4002. The Compass
and Chain

* *Also:* Crown of Thorns.

Non-Quilts

The following patterns technically are not quilts; they have no stuffing or lining, and are not quilted. Because they are popular among quilters, however, they are included here for identification.

1. Cathedral Windows
   Attic Windows

2. Variation of Cathedral Windows

3. Yo-yo
   Bon-bon
   Puff
   Powder Puff
   Pinwheel
   Bed of Roses
   Rosette

4. Martha Washington's Flower Garden (Yo-yos placed as in regular Flower Garden)

5. Yo-yo

6. Diamond Yo-yo

Suggested Reading

Bacon, Lenice I. *American Patchwork Quilts.* Morrow & Co., 1973.

Bannister, Barbara and Ford, Edna Paris. *State Capitals Quilt Blocks.* Dover, 1977.

Bannister, Barbara and Ford, Edna Paris. *The United States Patchwork Pattern Book.* Dover, 1976.

———. *Better Homes and Gardens Patchwork Pattern Book.* Dover, 1976.

Beyer, Jinny. *Patchwork Patterns.* EPM, 1979.

———. *The Quilter's Album of Blocks & Borders.* EPM, 1980.

Bishop, Robert and Safanda, Elizabeth. *A Gallery of Amish Quilts.* Dutton, 1976.

Brown, Elsa. *Creative Quilting.* Watson-Guptill, 1975.

Colby, Averill. *Patchwork Quilts.* Charles Scribner's Sons, 1965.

———. *Quilting.* Charles Scribner's Sons, 1971.

Echols, Margit. *The Quilter's Coloring Book.* Crowell, 1979.

Edwards, Phoebe. *Anyone Can Quilt.* Benjamin/Sterns and Foster Co., 1976.

Ericson, Helen. *Mrs. Danner's Quilts,* Books 1, 2, 3, 4. P. O. Box 650, Emporia, KS 66801.

———. *Helen's Book of Basic Quilt Making,* Book 7. P. O. Box 650, Emporia, KS 66801.

Finley, Ruth. *Old Patchwork Quilts and the Women Who Made Them.* Branford Co., 1929.

Frager, Dorothy. *The Quilting Primer.* Chilton, 1979.

Gammell, Alice. *Polly Prindle's Book of American Patchwork Quilts.* Grosset and Dunlap, 1973.

Gilberg, L. S. and Buchholz, B. B. *Needlepoint Designs from Amish Quilts.* Charles Scribner's Sons, 1977.

Green, Sylvia. *Patchwork for Beginners.* Watson-Guptill, 1972.

Gutcheon, Beth. *The Perfect Patchwork Primer.* Penguin Books, 1973.

Gutcheon, Beth and Jeffrey. *The Quilt Design Workbook.* Rawson Associates, 1976.

Hall, C. A. and Kretsinger, R. G. *The Romance of the Patchwork Quilt in America.* Bonanza, 1935.

Hinson, Delores. *A Quilter's Companion.* Arco, 1973.

———. *Quilting Manual.* Hearthside Press, 1966.

Houck, Carter and Miller, Myron. *American Quilts and How to Make Them.* Charles Scribner's Sons, 1975.

Ickis, M. *The Standard Book of Quilt Making and Collecting.* Dover, 1949.

Johnson, Mary Elizabeth. *Prize Country Quilts.* Oxmoor House, 1977.

Lady's Circle Patchwork Quilts. Lopez Publications, New York (published six times per year).

Larsen, Judith and Gull, Carol. *The Patchwork Quilt Design & Coloring Book.* Butterick, 1977.

Leman, Bonnie. *Quick and Easy Quilting.* Hearthside Press, 1972.

Levy, Judy. *Patchwork Pillows.* Dover, 1977.

Lewis, Alfred. *The Mountain Artisans Quilting Book.* Macmillan, 1973.

Lithgow, Marilyn. *Quiltmaking and Quiltmakers.* Funk & Wagnalls, 1974.

Malone, Maggie. *Classic American Patchwork Quilt Patterns.* Drake, 1977.

Mathieson, Elizabeth. *The Needlework Library.* World, 1949.

———. *The McCall's Book of Quilts.* Simon & Schuster, 1975.

———. *The McCall's Super-Book of Quilting.* McCall's, 1964.

McKim, Ruby. *101 Patchwork Patterns.* Dover, 1962.

Mills, Susan W. *Illustrated Index to Traditional American Quilt Patterns.* Arco, 1980.

Murwin, S. A. and Payne, S. C. *Quick and Easy Patchwork on the Sewing Machine.* Dover, 1979.

———. *Old-Fashioned Pieced and Appliqué Quilts.* Indiana Farmer's Guide, n. d.

———. *Old Time Needlecraft—Designs and Patterns.* House of White Birches, 1970.

Orlofsky, P. and Orlofsky, M. *Quilts in America.* McGraw-Hill, 1974.

Patchword, Hearthside Crafts Quilters Club (published four times per year). Edmonton, Alberta, Canada.

Patchwork Patter, National Quilters Association (published four times per year). Ellicott City, MD.

Quilt, Harris Publications, New York (published four times per year).

Quilter's Newsletter, Leman Publications, Wheatridge, Colorado (published ten times per year).

Quilt World and *Quilt World Omnibook*, House of White Birches, Seabrook, New Hampshire (published six times per year).

Stafford, C. L. and Bishop, R. *America's Quilts and Coverlets.* Weathervane Books, 1974.

Taylor, Sibby. *New and Easy Quilting.* Barnes & Co., 1977.

Timmons, Alice. *Patchwork Simplified.* Arco, 1973.

Vote, M. *Patchwork Pleasure—A Pattern Identification Guide.* Wallace-Homestead, n. d.

Weiss, Rita. *Easy-to-Make Patchwork Quilts.* Dover, 1978.

Wilson, Erica. *Quilts of America.* Oxmoor House, 1979.

Wooster, Ann-Sargent. *Quiltmaking—The Modern Approach to a Traditional Craft.* Drake, 1972.

Index

The number or numbers following each pattern name indicate the pattern number, not the page number. Many patterns have more than one name while others have only one. Some designs may share the same name with other designs.